DOCTOR'S ORDERS

DOCTOR'S ORDERS

Over 50 Inventive Cocktails to Cure, Revive & Enliven

Chris Edwards & Dave Tregenza

hardie grant books

CONTENTS

7 Introduction

8 Before You Start

Part One
THE SET UP

12 Spirits

14 Bar Necessities

16 Kit Bag

18 Bag of Tricks

20 Base Recipes

26 The Anatomy of A Drink

Part Two
THE RECIPES

30 REMEDIES

77 COMFORTERS

91 REVIVERS

121 RESTORE/RECTIFY

138 Cocktail Party Ideas

139 Index

143 About the Authors & Acknowledgements

INTRODUCTION

The recipes inside this book are inspired by the medicinal 'Doctor's Orders' cocktails served at both our bars. The recipes all have suggested benefits but these are a fun guide and should be taken as so.

The first part of this book, The Set Up is an introduction to the tools, equipment, and base bar ingredients you should have before you get started. This section also includes base recipes for bitters, tinctures, shrubs and syrups that will be used frequently in the cocktail recipes. The second part, The Recipes are just that.

All our drinks are inspired by fresh flavours and ingredients enhanced by infusions, cordials and shrubs. We also take a lot of inspiration from food and cooking techniques from around the world. We like the idea of interaction and theatre, whether that comes from a garnish or an accompaniment to the drink. Above all, we want to make tasty, interesting drinks that people come back for.

All of the recipes in this book can be made in a home kitchen using new but mostly old techniques. Yes, we use some gadgets and equipment such as smoking guns, but these items are commonplace now in bars and kitchens across the world. A dehydrator, you might ask? This is now widely used as a money-saving staple in bars as the answer to perishable garnishes. Some of our ideas are a little out there, but they can all be made simply and easily following the recipes provided.

When we decided to open our first bar in London, The Shrub and Shutter, we knew we wanted to make playful, crowd-pleasing drinks that incorporate shrubs. We used our rooftop herb garden and a culinary approach to inspire the fresh and innovative drinks.

The concept of our second place, The First Aid Box, is based on refreshing health-inspired drinks using superfoods, medicinal ingredients and doctors paraphernalia. The menu is divided up into Doctor's Orders and Against Doctor's Orders so the health conscious and not so can enjoy the drinks in equal measure.

Chris & Dave

BEFORE YOU START

Before you get started, make sure you read this page . . .

Doctor's Orders
The benefits of the drink (not medical advice).

Vitamins & Minerals
Explaining the super ingredients.

Style/Tasting Notes
To take you from home mixologist to cocktail connoisseur.

Perfect Serve
Recommended brands to use in the recipe. Feel free to use other brands if you prefer.

Ingredients
Everything you need to prepare the final result. Make sure to read the 'Prep' to see if you'll need to make any additional bitters, shrubs, syrups or tinctures before making the chosen cocktail. The numbers correspond to subrecipes in the 'Prep'.

Prep
Information for any ingredients that need to be prepared in advance. The numbers show you how these ingredients tie into the final result. The flask icon lets you know how early you'll need to start preparing the ingredients.

Serve
How to pull the whole thing together.

Garnish
Strictly optional, but adds that something extra. These notes tell you how to present the cocktails like we do in the bar.

Doctor's Note
Easier swaps and alternatives for when you need a quick fix.

Part One
THE SET UP

SPIRITS

Spirits are the cornerstone of every bar. Here are our favourite classic spirits and how best to use them:

Gin

A few different types should do, a London dry and perhaps a flavoured or herbaceous one. We suggest **Warner Edwards** varietals or **Gin Mare** respectively.

Navy Gin (overproof gin) is a must for the brave and stupid alike or for a navy gin martini – perfect for a gin style zombie. We suggest **Plymouth Navy Strength** or **Perry's Tot Navy Strength**.

Sloe gin is a must for millionaires, daises and negroni twists. We suggest **Cremorne Gentleman Badger's** or **Warner Edwards**.

Vodka

It's definitely worth having three levels of vodka. An entry level for mixing such as **Ketel One** or **Wry**, a premium like **Belvedere** for naked martinis and an overproof for making tinctures such as **Balkan 176°**.

Rum

Rum is super versatile and can work throughout the seasons. Overproof styles (with an alcohol content over 57.5 per cent) are fun for tiki-style drinks.

White rum is a staple for mojitos and daiquiris. We suggest **El Dorado** or **Cana Brava**.

Aged rums, such as **Ron Millonario Sistema Solera 15-Year** or **Diplomatico Reserva Exclusiva** are brilliant for negronis or old fashioned-style drinks.

Dark rum is needed for mixing tiki punches or dark and stormys. Its got to be **Gosling's** or **Myers's**.

Single Malt Scotch

A drink more popular straight or with ice or water, although delicious when stirred in old fashioneds or enhanced by smoke, fire or surprisingly with floral notes. Scotch lovers will have their favourites. for a point of difference we suggest smokiness, so an **Ardbeg**, **Laphroaig** or **Octomore**.

Blended Whisky

Usually sweeter and more rounded off than Scotch, so best for mixing with. An all-rounder is needed for different styles of drinks and for a straight up tipple. **Auchentoshan Three Wood** is our favourite or **Nikka From the Barrel** for a sweet but boozy blend.

Bourbon/Rye

Best known in old-fashioneds, sazeracs, juleps and sours, but should be used more in long drinks as its sweet, creamy notes work well with stone fruits, berries and herbs. **Rittenhouse** or **FEW** are our suggestions. **Sazerac** rye is also superb. It's important to have a few bourbons as well. **Maker's Mark**, **Woodford** or **Four Roses** are good starting points, then upgrade to **Blanton's** or **Smooth Ambler**.

Tequila

Tequila is underused in drinks outside its comfort zone, such as margaritas and palomas. It works best with fresh garden ingredients and savoury flavours, and is delicious infused. We suggest the **Ocho** or **Centinela** ranges.

Mescal

Always thought of as smoky tequila – but it is so much more, and came way before its better known cousin. Brilliant with spice, it works best with bitter mixers or super-clean flavours that need to be roughed up. If you have only one mescal get **Del Maguey Vida** as it packs a big upfront smokiness. Not all mescals are smoky. **Bruxo** is a smooth alternative but still smoky.

Brandy

Different brandies and styles yield very different results. Pisco, for example, works best in sours and punches, while cognac sits in the stirred drinks side of the cabinet. All brandies should be used more in mixed drinks. You need at least two – one cognac for sipping and sidecars and a pisco for sours. **Ysabel Regina** cognac is superb for the former and **Pisco El Gobernador** for the latter.

BAR NECESSITIES

Sure you might have spirits, but if you want to mix drinks you'll also need some liqueurs, vermouths or bitters at the very least, and some citrus and sweetness for balancing out.

Liqueurs or Eau de Vies
- Triple Sec or dry curaçao
- **Benedictine**
- Maraschino
- Strawberry, raspberry, violette, peach, cassis (**Briottet** range is our favourite)
- Chartreuse (yellow and green)
- Coffee liqueur – **Kalhua**, **Mr Blacks**
- Absinthe (get a good one like **St. George**)
- Dry, white, rose and red vermouth (**Cocchi** or **Belazar** ranges)

Aperitivos
- **Campari**
- **Aperol**
- **Picon**
- **Suze**

Bitters
Amaro di Angostura, Creole, barrel-aged, Abbott's, orange, celery, other fruits, droplets or make your own (see D.I.Y. bitters page 22–23)

Citrus
- Lemon
- Lime
- Pomelo
- Yellow or pink grapefruit
- Yuzu

Sweetness
- Agave
- Honey
- Maple
- Sugar syrup

Cordials & Syrups
- Elderflower
- Homemade flavours – rhubarb, vanilla

Toppers
- Soda water
- Tonic water
- Sparkling wine
- Beer: wheat, IPA

Freshness
Think fruit, herbs, flowers ... there are no boundaries or wrong answers. Have fun choosing your poisons!

KIT BAG

Essentials for home or on-the-move cocktail making are as follows.

Glassware
Ideally, a range including highballs, tankards, rocks glasses, martini glasses, coupes, and plastic cups.

Shakers
Different kinds for different people. We suggest a tin on tin shaker, as you can fit more than one drink inside and it is pretty much indestructible, unlike its glass brothers.

Strainers
It's worth investing in heavy-duty Hawthorn strainers for longevity. The better quality strainers have a longer and tighter spring to filter tightly when pouring ❶.

Double strain all drinks with fruit or herbs so you don't get debris in the drinks. Also double strain shaken drinks straight up to avoid chipped and broken up ice. Always try to use a strainer which curves into a point for an easier pour. See a CoCo strainer for a good example.

Jiggers (for measuring)
We suggest 25–50 ml (1–2 fl oz) jiggers. Try jiggers out for comfort, as an awkward jigger will make for an awkward-looking bartender ❷. Go for practical, not flashy.

Bar spoon
Needed for small measurements and, of course, stirring. The stronger the better. Length is key to adding theatre to your stir. ❸

Freezer
To store your ice and chill your glasses.

Straws
Something people forget!

Towels
Towels can act as your bar base where the action happens, meaning your bar can be almost anywhere.

Misc.
Bottle openers, pencil ❹, skewers, ice pick ❺, grater, scissors, tool bag ❻, citrus peeler ❼

BAG OF TRICKS

These tools are not musts, but it's always nice to have something up your sleeve. An element of theatre can elevate a drink from regular to crowd-pleasing.

Blowtorch

Our favourite. Fire up, heat, caramelise, smoke, spark, torch . . . the list is endless.

Smoking Gun

Not essential. The blowtorch can help with most smoky plans and is wonderful for creating theatre.

Cloche/Smoking Jar

Capture the smoke you have created.

Paint Brushes

Great for adding rims or powders on glasses with the help of a sticking agent such as agave or honey.

Overproof Spirits

These have a higher alcohol content and light quickly for fire and excitement.

Thermomix/Food Processor/Spice Grinder

For your own purées, sauces, powders and rims.

Dehydrator

A bar owner's best friend. Dehydrated garnishes are all the rage as they save on waste, look amazing and add texture and colour. The dehydrating possibilities are endless – think rims, edible garnishes, snacks, leathers or fruit.

BASE RECIPES

The measurements in this book are of an amount useful for making many drinks. should you want less or more divide or times the recipe to make a suitable amount for your needs.

Shrubs

Shrubs are effectively drinking vinegars, and go as far back as the 15th century. They were known as medicinal cordials and were used for preserving or adding acidic notes to soft drinks and punches.

To make a base shrub, any type of vinegar can be used. Choose vinegars based on the flavour you want to achieve: for example, a spiced apple shrub would work best with a cider vinegar, or rice wine vinegar would work well for a miso or soy shrub. Most of the shrubs used in this book use equal parts vinegar and syrup, but playing around with the ratios brings fun results should you desire a sharper, more tart shrub or a sweeter one.

The resting times given for shrubs in these recipes are the minimums. The key is to remove any fruit or herb that will change the colour if left in too long (e.g. fresh mint). Then, you can leave to age for as long as you desire.

WHITE WINE VINEGAR BASE SHRUB

400 ml (14 oz) white wine vinegar

400 ml (14 oz) sugar syrup

CIDER VINEGAR BASE SHRUB

400 ml (14 oz) cider vinegar

400 ml (14 oz) sugar syrup

Multiply or divide the ingredients based on how many batches you would like to make.

The amounts of shrub that go in any drink will obviously affect the taste greatly so also have a play around at the actual cocktail making stage.

Bitters

Adding bitters are a great way of imparting aromatics into a drink or enlivening a spirit's botanicals, flavours or character.

D.I.Y. Bitters

If you're making your own bitters, first think about what flavour you're after and adapt your base spirit to that flavour. Clean flavours = vodka. Spice = tequila, rum or whisky. Smoke = whisky, tequila or mescal. See page 24 for suggested base spirits. Alternatively, make your base bitters with a neutral spirit like vodka and then add different fruits or introduce other spirits.

BASE BITTER RECIPE

This recipe below can be the base from which to launch your bitters.

400 ml (14 fl oz) base overproof spirit

dried zests/peels of 6 lemons, 6 limes, 6 oranges, 4 pink grapefruits

1 cinnamon stick

3 allspice berries

10 pink peppercorns

1 heaped teaspoon dried gentian root

1 heaped teaspoon dried orris root

1 heaped teaspoon dried dandelion root

1 heaped teaspoon dried burdock root

1 heaped teaspoon dried angelica root

20 ml (½ oz) sugar syrup

Add all the ingredients to a 1 litre (35 oz) swingtop jar. Pour your chosen base overproof spirit into the jar. Leave to rest for 4–6 weeks, shaking every week. Fine strain through a muslin and decant into dropper or bitter bottles.

CHERRY BITTERS

700 ml (25 oz) base bitters using navy strength gin (see left)

100 ml (3½ oz) cherry brandy

20 fresh black cherries halved

Add all the ingredients to a 1 litre (35 oz) jar. Leave to rest for 4–6 weeks shaking every week. Fine strain through a muslin and decant into dropper or bitter bottles.

GINGER BITTERS

700 ml (25 oz) base bitters using overproof rum (see left)

500 g of fresh peeled and sliced ginger

1 bruised and bashed stick of lemongrass

1 star anise

1 heaped teaspoon of dried chilli flakes

Add all the ingredients to a 1 litre (35 oz) jar. Leave to rest for 4–6 weeks, shaking every week. Fine strain through a muslin and decant into dropper or bitter bottles.

CELERY BITTERS

700 ml (25 oz) base bitters using overproof vodka (see left)

1 finely chopped bunch or head of celery

1 finely sliced green apple

25 g (2 tsp) lovage leaves

1 thumb of finely chopped fresh peeled ginger

Add all the ingredients to a 1 litre (35 oz) jar. Leave to rest for 4–6 weeks shaking every week. Fine strain through a muslin and decant into dropper or bitter bottles.

Base Tinctures

Tinctures are easier to make than bitters as the process is effectively infusion.

A tincture can be made by simply adding an ingredient – whether it be a fruit, herb, spice or flavour – into a spirit.

Our recommendations for tincture bases are as follows:

Vodka
Balkan 176° Vodka

Gin
Plymouth Navy Gin

Rum
Wray & Nephew Overproof Rum

Bourbon
Few Cask Strength Bourbon

Whisky
Red Breast 12-Year Cask Strength

Rye
Rittenhouse Straight Rye Whisky 100 Proof

Simply place your chosen ingredients in a sterilised jar. Pour over your chosen spirit and leave to stand for 2–3 weeks, shaking occasionally in order to maximise the flavour.

One ingredient is fun, but the more the merrier.

Sugar Syrup

To make sugar syrup, mix equal quantities of sugar and water in a saucepan. Bring to the boil, then heat for 3 minutes until the sugar has dissolved. Leave to cool and pour into a sterilised bottle or jar. Store in the fridge for up to one month.

THE ANATOMY OF A DRINK

The perfect prescription.

Bartenders or mixologists will tell you there is an art to making drinks and this is true, to a point. But anyone can make a drink: it's just about loosening up and not being embarrassed by doing it. It's like dad dancing – don't be awkward, just throw yourself into it.

Shaking

Everyone's been there, shaking a cocktail and looking embarrassed. Don't be. The reason for shaking a cocktail is to aerate the drink, break down any fruit or other ingredients, to chill the drink and to dilute. Shake hard and in a circular motion and you're there. Any other tricks are just for show-offs.

Stirring

Stirring is done to chill a drink. A stirred drink rarely has fruit or any other ingredient aside from liquids in it. The vigorous action of shaking is therefore not needed to rapidly break down the mix; instead, the stirring action dilutes and chills at the same time. Stirring well is about rhythm.

Garnishing

After your drink is poured into its vessel, it usually needs a garnish. The simplest garnish is a fruit peel, whether lemon, lime or pink grapefruit. Oil can be extracted or expressed from the peel with a simple squeeze to release. The oils released will settle on the top of the drink as an aroma. The peel can also be wiped around the rim for taste when drinking.

Garnishes can be as weird and wonderful as you like, and there are no rules. Food, sweets, fire, smoke . . . all can become garnishes to enhance a drink or add an element of fun.

Skewers can also be used to attach garnishes to drinks in all manner of ways.

Part Two
THE RECIPES

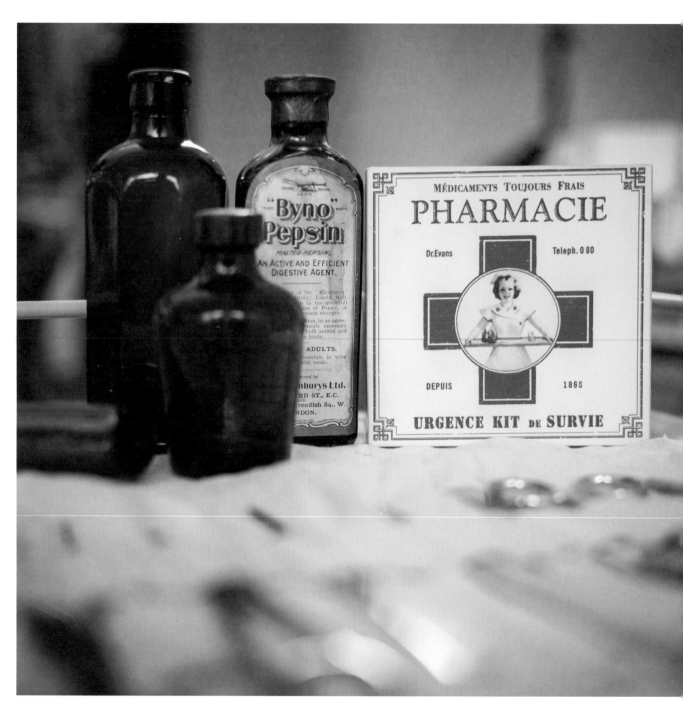

REMEDIES

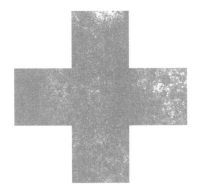

The drinks in this chapter were all created with health in mind. Of course, any drink with alcohol isn't going to be completely virtuous, but these tipples will ease the guilt, at least.

When we opened First Aid Box we decided we wanted to use superfoods and superfruits in our drinks – ingredients that would enhance other flavours, botanicals, spices as well as lend a healthy streak to the cocktails.

The recipes in this chapter will cleanse, refresh and make you feel good. They are especially good as aperitifs or palate cleansers.

BEETS BY WRAY

Witness the fitness. An earthy, raw and root-based twist on a Daiquiri.

Doctor's Orders:
blood flow, stamina, brain power

Vitamins & Minerals:
nitrates

Style/Tasting Notes:
earthy Hemingway daiquiri

Glass/Vessel:
large coupe

Perfect Serve:
Capucana Cachaça, Wray & Nephew Overproof Rum

Ingredients

40 ml (1½ oz) beetroot-infused cachaça or white rum ❶ or use 50 ml (1¾ oz) of base spirit

10 ml (⅓ oz) overproof rum (optional)

15 ml (½ oz) Maraschino

25 ml (1 oz) vanilla sugar or vanilla-infused sugar syrup

25 ml (1 oz) cloudy apple juice

25 ml (1 oz) fresh lime juice

Prep

❶ Add 1 sliced, cooked beetroot to a 700 ml (28 oz) bottle of cachaça or white rum. Leave for at least 2 hours. This will make enough for 14 drinks.

Serve

Add all the ingredients to a shaker with ice. Shake hard and double strain into a large coupe over chipped ice.

PREP 2 HOURS AHEAD

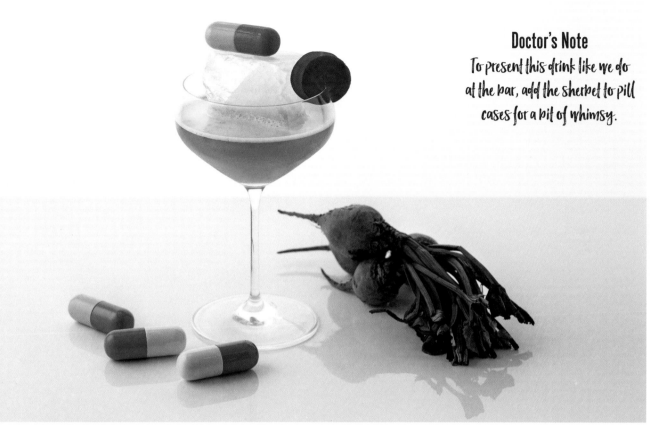

Garnish

Store-bought lemon or beetroot sherbet; beetroot crisp (if desired)

To make beetroot sherbet, put the grated zest of 2 lemons and 2 thinly sliced, cooked beetroots into a dehydrator until both are crisp. Blend dried lemon and beetroot into a powder then add 100 g (3½ oz) caster sugar and 1 tablespoon citric acid until completely mixed. Add the beetroot sherbet to the pill cases for service, if desired.

To make beetroot crisps, preheat the oven to 60°C (160°F/Gas 0). Slice a cooked beetroot thinly on a mandolin. Lay the slices on a tray and bake until crisp. Alternatively, use a dehydrator if you have one.

Garnish
Toasted almonds, sliced kiwi (if desired)

DR SEUSS

Enter a healthy and wonderful world of Dr Seuss madness.

Ingredients

50 ml (1¾ oz) kiwi infused gin ❶

50 ml (1¾ oz) strawberry and thyme juice ❷

20 ml (¾ oz) kaffir lime syrup ❸

6 slices of fresh kiwi (2 for garnished skewer, if desired)

25 ml (1 oz) fresh lime juice

cucumber and watermelon tonic water

Prep

❶ Peel and slice 2 kiwis and add to a jar filled with a 700 ml (28 oz) bottle of gin. Leave to infuse for at least 2 days.

❷ Add 1 kilo of strawberries, 1 bunch of fresh thyme and 100 ml of mineral water to a saucepan over a medium heat. Bring to a boil and then reduce to a low heat and simmer until all the fruit has broken down to a pulp. Let cool before straining the mix through a sieve.

❸ Add 6 kaffir lime leaves to 500 ml (18 oz) of hot sugar syrup. Leave to cool then strain.

Serve

Add all the ingredients expect the tonic water to a shaker, shake hard and single strain into a glass filled with ice and 4 slices of fresh kiwi. Top with the cucumber and watermelon tonic water and more ice if needed. Ensure all the fresh kiwi slices are spread around the glass by churning with a bar spoon.

Doctor's Orders:
skin care

Vitamins & Minerals:
vitamins C, E & K, manganese, copper, folate, potassium

Style/Tasting Notes:
clean flavours, upfront fruitiness, tart and sweet in equal measures, layers of flavour

Glass/Vessel:
bamboo cooler

Perfect Serve:
Oxley Gin, Double Dutch Cucumber and Watermelon Tonic Water

INSTANT CURE

Doctor's Orders:
energy, muscle strength

Vitamins & Minerals:
iodine, vitamins A and
C, calcium

Style/Tasting Notes:
smoky, peaty, salty

Glass/Vessel:
simple rocks glass

Perfect Serve:
Nikka From the Barrel
Whisky

SMOKE THE WEED

A peaty, vegetal, earthy negroni which will leave you on a high.

Ingredients

25 ml (1 oz) peaty or smoky whisky

15 ml (½ oz) Cynar

15 ml (½ oz) Campari

10 ml (⅓ oz) store-bought dashi or seaweed stock ❶

5 ml (⅕ oz) sugar syrup (see page 24)

pink grapefruit peel

Prep

❶ If making the seaweed stock, take 60 g (2 oz) of dried shiitake mushrooms, cover with water and bring to the boil. Add 6 nori seaweed sheets and stir until dissolved and infused. Add 1 tablespoon of dark soy sauce. Simmer until the mixture has reduced by half. This will last for a week in the fridge and makes 10 drinks.

Serve

Add all the ingredients to a stirring glass filled with ice. Stir until sufficiently chilled. Single strain into a simple rocks glass over chipped ice. Twist a pink grapefruit peel over the top of the drink, then rim the glass with the peel.

PREP
2 HOURS
AHEAD

Garnish

Store-bought kale crisps (chips) or dehydrated soy-glazed kale crisps (if desired) ❷ served in a bag; mini clothes peg.

❷ To make the soy-glazed kale crisps, preheat the oven to 60°C (140°F/ Gas 1). Take 500 kg (18 oz) of kale and wash thoroughly. Pat the kale dry, and then lay the kale leaves on a baking tray. Take a brush and glaze each leaf with soy sauce. Bake for about 2 hours until crisp, then bag up the leaves for serving. Alternatively, use a dehydrator if you've got one.

Doctor's Note

You can buy kale crisps at most supermarkets if you don't have time to make them. Alternatively, enjoy the drink without the crisps.

Garnish

Lightly pickled cucumber slice (if desired)

Dip a cucumber slice in the cucumber shrub.

Doctor's Note

For an instant cure, use gherkin pickle brine instead of the cucumber shrub.

CUCUMBER DAIQUIRI

A super cleansing, refreshing and revitalising martini – like going to the spa for a face mask.

Ingredients

60 ml (2 oz) white rum

15 ml (½ oz) fresh cucumber water ❶, or ¼ cucumber, muddled

5 ml (⅕ oz) cucumber shrub ❷

1 pinch of sea salt

1 grind of cracked black pepper

25 ml (1 oz) fresh lime juice

15 ml (½ oz) sugar syrup (see page 24)

Prep

❶ Using a juice extractor, juice 1 peeled cucumber (approx 100 ml (3½ oz) of juice).

❷ If making the shrub, start with one batch of base shrub mix (see page 20) using half cider vinegar and half white wine vinegar. Add 2 thinly sliced cucumbers to the mix and leave for at least 2 days. This will last for 3–6 months and make 60 drinks.

Serve

Add all the ingredients to a shaker. Shake hard with ice and double strain into a martini glass.

Doctor's Orders:
cleanse, digestion, hydration, skin health

Vitamins & Minerals:
vitamins C and K

Style/Tasting Notes:
super fresh, clean, spring water

Glass/Vessel:
martini glass

Perfect Serve:
Banks 5 Island Rum

PREP 2 DAYS AHEAD

Doctor's Orders:
electricity, immune boost

Vitamins & Minerals:
iron, vitamins B, C and D

Style/Tasting Notes:
natural, fresh, zing

Glass/Vessel:
rocks

Perfect Serve:
Vulson Old Rhino Rye Whisky

PREP
2 DAYS
AHEAD

FIELD NOTES

An earthy cocktail that could have been lifted from a forager's journal.

Ingredients

50 ml (2 oz) Périgord black-truffle-infused whisky ❶

10 ml (⅓ oz) Yellow Chartreuse

20 ml (¾ oz) field mushroom syrup ❷

20 ml (¾ oz) fresh lemon juice

1 egg white

Prep

❶ Shave approximately 12 slices of Périgord black truffle and add to a 700 ml (28 oz) bottle of whisky. Leave for at least 2 days to infuse. This will make enough for 14 drinks.

❷ If making the syrup, add 200 g (7 oz) of field mushrooms and 300 g (17½ oz) of caster sugar to a pan and heat slowly. Add 300 ml (17½ oz) of water regularly then let simmer until you have a light mushroom-flavoured syrup. Strain mushrooms through a sieve. The syrup will last in the fridge for a week and makes 25 drinks.

Serve

Add all the ingredients to a shaker and shake the mix. Then add ice to the shaker and shake hard. Single strain over ice into a rocks glass.

Doctor's Note
For a slightly less decadant drink, use thinned-out truffle honey instead of the field mushroom syrup.

Garnish
Dushi button and shaved Périgord black truffle (if desired)

Garnish

Half a bourbon fig (if desired)

To make bourbon figs, slice 10 figs in half and steep in
200 ml (7 oz) of bourbon. Use when needed. Pat before use.

Doctor's Note

Feel free to use fresh
ginger instead of ginger
bitters – just remember
to double strain.

BALL PARK FIGURE

The smoky fig aromas lend this cocktail a festive air.

Ingredients

25 ml (1 oz) smoky or peaty whisky

25 ml (1 oz) bourbon

½ fresh fig, muddled

3 drops ginger bitters (see page 23), or ½ thumb fresh ginger, muddled

3 drops Angostura bitters

10 ml (⅓ oz) sugar syrup (see page 24)

orange peel

Serve

Add all the ingredients to a stirring glass filled with ice. Stir until the mix is sufficiently chilled. Single strain (or double strain if using ginger) over chipped ice into a tumbler. Twist the orange peel over the drink.

PREP
1 WEEK
AHEAD

Doctor's Orders:
development, wisdom, antiseptic

Vitamins & Minerals:
vitamin C

Style/Tasting Notes:
nuclear, smoky, herbal

Glass/Vessel:
drip bag or highball

Perfect Serve:
Star of Bombay Gin

THIRST AID

A nuclear and herbalist smoky gin sour.

Ingredients

50 ml (2 oz) dry gin

10 ml (⅓ oz) smoky mescal

10 ml (⅓ oz) Green Chartreuse

5 fresh sage leaves

5 fresh mint leaves

150 ml (5 oz) fresh or store-bought pineapple juice (not from concentrate)

25 ml (1 oz) fresh lemon juice

20 ml (¾ oz) elderflower cordial

Serve

Multiply the recipe quantities by the number of drinks you would like to make. Add all the ingredients to a large storage jar, stir and leave all the flavours to infuse for 10 minutes before straining the herbs from the mix. Then fill drip bags individually, if using, and refrigerate ready for serving. To serve, add drip bag to stand and roll over to the patient. Alternatively, simply pour the mix into highball glasses.

INSTANT CURE

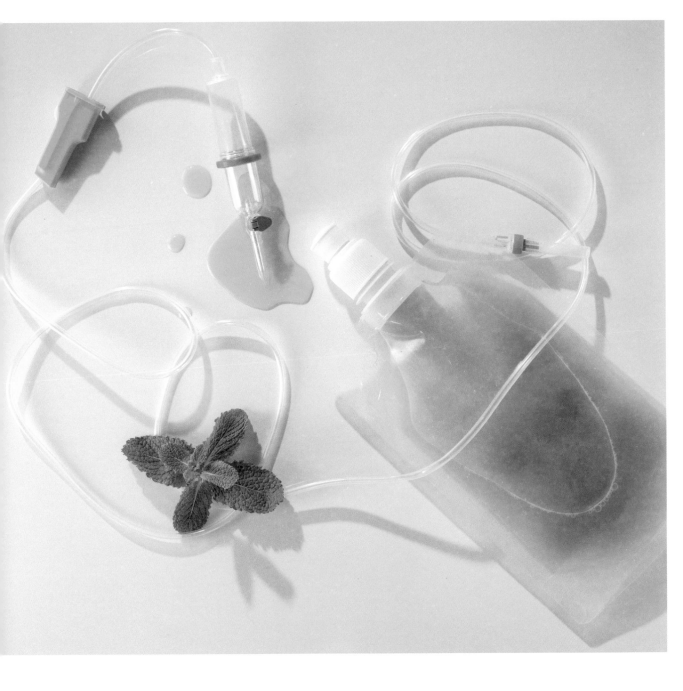

Garnish
Mini crab apple (if desired)

AN APPLE A DAY

An orchard-inspired thirst quencher for cider lovers.

Ingredients

15 ml (½ oz) Cognac

15 ml (½ oz) calvados

20 ml (¾ oz) green apple shrub ❶

1 teaspoon lemon sherbet, lemon juice or Salts of the Earth electric avenue tincture ❷

20 ml (¾ oz) cloudy apple juice

15 ml (½ oz) sugar

15 ml (½ oz) lemon juice

soda water, to top

Prep

❶ Add 4 sliced Granny Smith apples and 1 cinnamon stick to a large Kilner jar with 800 ml (28 oz) of cider vinegar base shrub mix (see page 20). Leave to infuse for at least 2 days. The shrub will keep for 3–6 months and makes 40 drinks.

❷ If making the tincture, add 100 g (3½ oz) of super sour apple sweets (hard candies) to 300 ml (10½ oz) of vodka. Then add 50 ml (2 oz) of fresh yuzu juice, 1 sprig of lemon thyme and 25 g (1 oz) of citric acid. Stir the mixture until the sweets and citric acid have diluted. Strain the liquid through a muslin. Feel free to add more citric acid for added electric zip.

Serve

Add all the ingredients to a shaker. Shake and single strain into a soda stream bottle. Then soda stream the mixture in the bottle to add CO_2 fizz. Pour over ice into a wide highball and garnish with a mini crab apple. If you don't have a soda stream, simply top with soda water.

Doctor's Orders:
energy, hydration, digestion

Vitamins & Minerals:
vitamin C, phytonutrients, antioxidant, fibre

Style/Tasting Notes:
cider replacement, fresh, long with a sour kick

Glass/Vessel:
wide highball

Perfect Serve:
Balkan 176° Vodka, Baron de Sigognac 10-Year Cognac, Berneroy XO Calvados

REMEDIES

PREP 2 DAYS AHEAD

Doctor's Orders:
antiseptic

Vitamins & Minerals:
vitamin C

Style/Tasting Notes:
floral, herbal, vibrant

Glass/Vessel:
tapered highball

Perfect Serve:
Forest Gin

PREP
2 DAYS
AHEAD

PARKLIFE

A boozy elderflower pressé which explodes with country flavours.

Ingredients

40 ml (1½ oz) gin

10 ml (⅓ oz) St-Germain elderflower liqueur

10 ml (⅓ oz) Yellow Chartreuse

15 ml (½ oz) Brockwell Park elderflower shrub ❶

20 ml (¾ oz) fresh lemon juice

10 ml (⅓ oz) sugar syrup (see page 24)

soda water, to top

Prep

❶ Add 100 g (3½ oz) of elderflower cordial to 600 ml (21 oz) of white wine vinegar base shrub mix (see page 20). Leave the mix for at least 2 days before serving. It will last for 3–6 months and makes 40 drinks.

Serve

Add all the ingredients except the soda to a shaker filled with ice. Shake hard and double strain into a tapered highball filled with ice. Top with ice and soda to the brim. Mix the drink with a bar spoon to integrate the soda.

Garnish
Freshly picked
elderflowers
(if desired)

Garnish

Pickled rhubarb slices on a fork skewer; red vein sorrel cress (if desired)

To make pickled rhubarb, thinly slice a stick of fresh rhubarb and leave in a pickling liquor of 100 ml (3½ oz) of white wine vinegar, 50 ml (2 oz) of sugar syrup, 3 thyme sprigs and 20 pink peppercorns.

R+H+U+B+A+R+B

A quintessentially English, rhubarb-flavoured slap around the face.

Doctor's Orders:
skin health, digestion,
bone growth

Vitamins & Minerals:
vitamins B, C and K,
calcium

Style/Tasting Notes:
tart, pickled, sweet

Glass/Vessel:
vintage rocks

Perfect Serve:
Warner Edwards Dry
Gin, Victoria's Rhubarb
Gin, Fee Brothers
Rhubarb Bitters

Ingredients

25 ml (1 oz) gin

25 ml (1 oz) rhubarb gin, or
ordinary gin

5 ml (⅕ oz) Zucca-Rabarbara or
Campari

15 ml (½ oz) rhubarb shrub ❶

3 drops rhubarb bitters

25 ml (1 oz) fresh lemon juice

20 ml (¾ oz) sugar syrup (see
page 24)

1 egg white

Prep

❶ Slice 6 sticks of rhubarb into quarters, and add them to a pan with 400 ml (14 oz) of cider vinegar base shrub mix (see page 20). Heat the mix until the rhubarb breaks down. Sieve the mix to leave just the newly formed shrub. This will last 3–6 months and makes 38 drinks.

Serve

Add all the ingredients to a shaker and shake. Then add ice and wet shake hard. Single strain into a rocks glass over ice.

PREP
2 DAYS
AHEAD

POLLEN COUNT

A floral sour which conjures an English country garden.

Doctor's Orders:
sleep aid, energy, hay fever distraction

Vitamins & Minerals:
vitamin C

Style/Tasting Notes:
floral, aromatic, fresh, succulent

Glass/Vessel:
Champagne coupe

Perfect Serve:
Snow Queen Organic Vodka, Briottet Violette liqueur

Ingredients

35 ml (1¼ oz) vodka

10 ml (⅓ oz) violet liqueur

10 ml (⅓ oz) Dolin de Coeur Genepi

5 ml (⅕ oz) Bigallet Thym Liqueur

10 ml (⅓ oz) lavender shrub ❶

6 lemon verbena, lemon balm or fresh mint leaves

20 ml (¾ oz) honey

15 ml (½ oz) fresh lemon juice

1 egg white

Prep

❶ Add 1 bunch of lavender to a 1-litre (35-oz) Kilner jar with 400 ml (14 oz) of base shrub mix (see page 20), using half cider vinegar and half white wine vinegar. Leave to infuse for at least 1 day before it's ready to serve. Makes 80 drinks.

Serve

Add all the ingredients to a shaker and shake, then add ice and shake hard. Double strain mix into a Champagne coupe.

PREP
1 DAY
AHEAD

Garnish

Bee pollen and raspberry dust using a beehive-inspired stencil (hexagon stencil – can be bought online) (if desired)

To make the dust, take a punnet of raspberries and lay them on a dehydrating tray. Dehydrate until completely dried out and crisp before blitzing in a spice blender. Store in a dry container.

Garnish

Baby carrots with fresh mint tips; baby rhubarb cress (if desired)

At the bar, we serve with pea purée 'dip' (like the killer substance in the film).

WHO FRAMED ROGER RABBIT?

A vegetal and meadow-sweet spiced Collins.

Ingredients

40 ml (1½ oz) gin

10 ml (⅓ oz) Suze or dry vermouth

2 dashes celery bitters (see page 23 for homemade version)

25 ml (1 oz) shop-bought ginger syrup or ginger and roasted meadow hay syrup ❶

25 ml (1 oz) fresh lemon juice

15 ml (½ oz) carrot and celery shrub ❷

tonic water, to top

Prep

❶ If making ginger and roasted hay syrup, add 2 thumbs of peeled and sliced ginger to 900 ml (32 oz) of hot sugar syrup (see page 24). Roast 500 g (17½ oz) of meadow hay in a medium oven for 5 minutes. Add to the ginger syrup. Leave to cool then strain. The syrup will last a week in the fridge and makes 34 drinks.

❷ Add 12 carrots of different shapes, sizes and colours (including the tops), 4 large sticks of celery, 2 opened cardamom pods and 1 star anise to a jar of 800 ml (28 oz) of base cider vinegar shrub (see page 20). Leave for 2 days to infuse.

Serve

Shake all the ingredients together except the tonic. Single strain into the highball glass and top with tonic water.

Doctor's Orders:
cleanse, vision, weight loss, digestion, enhances animation

Vitamins & Minerals:
vitamin C, antioxidant

Style/Tasting Notes:
earthy, spicy yet cleaning

Glass/Vessel:
highball

Perfect Serve:
Bitter Truth Celery Bitters, Warner Edwards Dry Gin

REMEDIES

PREP
2 DAYS
AHEAD

DR GREENTHUMB

Take a trip to the doctor's greenhouse.

Ingredients

50 ml (2 oz) gin

10 ml (⅓ oz) Green Chartreuse

75 ml (2¾ oz) cucumber juice

25 ml (1 oz) minted pea shrub ❶

20 ml (¾ oz) pea purée ❷

25 ml (1 oz) fresh lime juice

20 ml (¾ oz) sugar syrup (see page 24)

Garnish

Nasturtium, dill, fennel cress and samphire (if desired)

Prep

❶ Add 250 g (9 oz) of garden peas and 1 bunch of fresh mint, to 600 ml (21 oz) of white wine vinegar shrub mix (see page 20), stir and leave overnight. Strain the mix. This will last for 3 months and makes 24 drinks.

❷ Take 500 g (17½ oz) of garden peas and blend in a Thermomix or food processor with 100 ml (3½ oz) of fresh lemon juice and a large pinch of salt. Add a splash of water if needed. Pour into a plastic squeezy bottle and keep refrigerated. Use the same day.

Serve

Add all the ingredients to a shaker with ice and shake hard. Double strain the mix into a conical flask filled with ice or a highball glass.

Doctor's Orders:
cleanse, digestion, antiseptic, skincare, manganese

Vitamins & Minerals:
vitamins C and K, calcium

Style/Tasting Notes:
cleansing, vegetal, refreshing

Glass/Vessel:
conical flask 500 ml (17½ oz)

Perfect Serve:
Gin Mare

PREP
1 DAY
AHEAD

Doctor's Orders:
awaken the eyes,
refresh, antioxidant

Vitamins & Minerals:
vitamin C

Style/Tasting Notes:
super fresh, acidic but
cleansing

Glass/Vessel:
Champagne coupe

Perfect Serve:
St. George Agricole Rum
or El Dorado 3-Year Rum

DRUGSTORE COWBOY

A wild west prescription.

Ingredients

½ star fruit

50 ml (2 oz) agricole rum or
white rum

10 ml (⅓ oz) aloe vera juice

4 fresh mint leaves

3 drops cardamom bitters or 1
cardamom pod, muddled

20 ml (¾ oz) fresh lime juice

¼ teaspoon of ascorbic acid or
20 ml (¾ oz) fresh lime juice

20 ml (¾ oz) honey water ❶

Prep
❶ Add boiling water to honey, just enough to loosen
and make it easy to pour from a bottle.

Serve
Muddle the star fruit in a shaker tin until the fruit
turns into a pulp. Add the rest of the ingredients and
shake hard. Double strain into a Champagne coupe.

INSTANT
CURE

Garnish

Star fruit slice and 2 slices of frozen aloe vera for soothing your eyes
(if desired)

Garnish

Spinach, paprika, sugar and salt rim (if desired)

To make the spiced rim mixture, preheat the oven to 60°C (140°F/Gas 1). Lay 500 g (17½ oz) of spinach on a tray and bake for about 2 hours until dried out. Add the dried spinach to a spice blender with 100 g (3½ oz) of sea salt and caster sugar with half a teaspoon of paprika. Blend make a dust and keep in a dry container for serving. Alternatively, omit the dried spinach and blend the remaining spices. To apply the spiced rim, take a small paintbrush and dip it into the agave syrup. Paint the glass with the syrup where you would like your spice rim. Dip the painted area into the spice mix and shake off the excess.

PAPAYA THE SAILORMAN

A travelling daiquiri meets a margarita.

Ingredients

25 ml (1 oz) agave syrup

25 ml (1 oz) mescal

25 ml (1 oz) rum

25 ml (1 oz) blanco tequila

25 ml (1 oz) store-bought or fresh papaya purée ❶

25 ml (1 oz) fresh lime juice

Prep

❶ Peel and deseed a papaya. Blend the flesh with 20 ml (¾ oz) of sugar syrup (see page 24) and a splash of water to loosen the mix.

Serve

Add all the ingredients to a shaker filled with ice. Shake hard and double strain into the rimmed Champagne coupe and serve.

PREP 2 HOURS AHEAD

Doctor's Orders:
brightness

Vitamins & Minerals:
vitamins A, C and B1,
copper, magnesium,
quinine

Style/Tasting Notes:
pure, fresh, exotic,
simple

Glass/Vessel:
16-oz (450-ml) takeaway
cup with dome lid or
large highball

Perfect Serve:
Whitley Neill Dry
Gin, Fee Brothers
Rhubarb Bitters, Double
Dutch Watermelon &
Cucumber Tonic

WATERMELON G&T

Holiday G&T, summer in a plastic glass.

Ingredients
1/16 of a watermelon, sliced
50 ml (1¾ oz) gin
3 drops rhubarb bitters
125 ml (1 oz) tonic water

Serve
Fill the glass with ice and watermelon slices, and then add the gin, rhubarb bitters and tonic water. Churn through the glass with a bar spoon to chill the drink before adding more ice.

INSTANT
CURE

Garnish
Sliced watermelon (if desired)

Garnish
Army soldier, fun snap bangers for added effect (if desired)

BANDAGE OF BROTHERS

World War-inspired medicinal martini – a perfect painkiller.

Ingredients

40 ml (1½ oz) vodka

15 ml (½ oz) poppy liqueur

10 ml (⅓ oz) Wolfschmidt Kummel

15 ml (½ oz) fresh lemon juice

10 ml (⅓ oz) sugar syrup (see page 24)

¼ bar spoon citric acid

Serve

Shake all the ingredients in a shaker filled with ice. Double strain into a martini glass.

(see page 24)

Doctor's Orders:
lower cholesterol, digestion

Vitamins & Minerals:
vitamin C, antioxidant

Style/Tasting Notes:
acidic, floral

Glass/Vessel:
crystal cut Martini

Perfect Serve:
Snow Queen Organic Vodka, Briottet Coquelicot de Nemours (Poppy) Liqueur

INSTANT CURE

JUNGLE FEVER

A Thai-inspired pina colada.

Doctor's Orders:
metabolism, immune system boost, memory, energy

Vitamins & Minerals:
vitamin E

Style/Tasting Notes:
spicy pina colada, curry flavours

Glass/Vessel:
bamboo cooler

Perfect Serve:
Rumbullion! Rum

Ingredients

60 ml (2 oz) rum

1 bar spoon high-quality store-bought Thai red curry paste or red jungle curry paste ❶

75 ml (2¾ oz) coconut water

25 ml (1 oz) coconut milk

2 chilli droplets or 1 pinch chilli flakes

2 ginger droplets or ½ thumb fresh ginger, muddled

20 ml (¾ oz) fresh lime

20 ml (¾ oz) ginger and lemongrass cordial

Prep

❶ If making curry paste, add to a blender: 2 sliced sticks lemongrass, 1 thumb of peeled galangal, 1 thumb of fresh ginger, half a medium red onion, 1 large teaspoon of dried red chilli flakes, 1 whole red chilli, 4 kaffir lime leaves, 2 tablespoons of dark soy sauce, 1 teaspoon of fish sauce, 1 teaspoon of coriander seeds, 1 tablespoon of tamarind paste, 25 ml (1 oz) of fresh lime juice, 1 tablespoon of palm sugar and a handful of coriander leaves and stalks. Blend until the mix turns into a paste. Then pour the paste into a jar for serving.

Serve

Add all the ingredients to a shaker with ice and shake hard. Strain mix into a bamboo cooler.

INSTANT CURE

Garnish

Lemongrass stalk, chopped lemongrass, fresh chilli, palm tree stirrer, lemongrass, honey and coconut lip balm (if desired)

To make lip balm, add 10 tablespoons of grated beeswax, 5 tablespoons of virgin coconut oil, 5 drops of lemongrass essential oil, 1 large tablespoon of raw organic honey and 20 vitamin E capsules to a pan. Heat all the ingredients and mix thoroughly. Carefully pour into lip balm cases or apothecary jars and leave to set.

Garnish
Shiso leaf, amaranth cress and sea bass sashimi with soy brush
(if desired)

Add a shiso leaf on a splitter skewer to the side of the teacup.

Doctors Note
To garnish like we do in the bar,
serve with a slice of sea bass sashimi
brushed with soy on a bed of
amaranth cress.

JIRO DREAMS OF SUSHI

A delicious trip to the fountain of youth.

Ingredients

40 ml (1½ oz) gin with cucumber notes

20 ml (¾ oz) Daiginjo Akashi-Tai

10 ml (⅓ oz) miso shrub ❶

3 drops wasabi tincture ❷

Lemon oil

Prep

❶ Add 2 large tablespoons of miso paste into mixing bowl with 100 ml (3½ oz) of boiling water. Mix and then add 600 ml (21 oz) base shrub mix (see page 20), using rice vinegar. Mix until all the miso paste has integrated into the liquid. Leave the mix for at least 2 days before straining through a muslin.

❷ Add 100 g (3½ oz) of freshly grated wasabi into a small jar. Add 100 ml (3½ oz) of vodka over the wasabi and leave for at least 2 days. Strain or keep the wasabi in the mix longer to infuse more.

Serve

Add all the ingredients into a stirring glass with ice and stir until sufficiently chilled. Single strain mix straight into a Japanese teacup, or other teacup, squeeze the lemon oil over the cup and rim the sides.

Vitamins & Minerals:
vitamins C, K and B5, potassium, calcium, iron

Style/Tasting Notes:
cleansing, pure, fresh, miso

Glass/Vessel:
Japanese teacup with slate Japanese serving plate

Perfect Serve:
Hendrick's Gin or Martin Miller's Gin, Balkan 176° Vodka

REMEDIES

PREP 2 DAYS AHEAD

Doctor's Orders:
immune boost, cold cure, hangover cure, energy boost, glow

Vitamins & Minerals:
all the vitamins

Style/Tasting Notes:
6 different fruits in one drink

Glass/Vessel:
large wine glass

Perfect Serve:
El Dorado 3-year Cask Aged Rum, Del Maguey VIDA Mescal, Les vergers Boiron strawberry purée, Les vergers Boiron mango purée

INSTANT CURE

CAPTAIN PLANET

A real hero, this superfruit punch is out of this world.

Ingredients
50 ml (1¾ oz) rum

20 ml (¾ oz) mescal

20 ml (¾ oz) moa superfood drink

30 ml (1 oz) strawberry purée

30 ml (1 oz) mango purée

50 ml (1¾ oz) coconut milk

1 kiwi fruit

2 fresh passion fruits

25 ml (1 oz) fresh lime juice

25 ml (1 oz) agave syrup

Serve
Add half of the rum, half of the mescal and all of the fresh lime juice and agave syrup into the bottom of the glass. Fill the glass with crushed ice to three-quarters of the way up the glass. Carefully add the 2 purées and coconut milk using squeeze bottles for each to different sections of the glass dispersing each through the crushed ice. Top the glass with ice before adding the other half of the rum and the other half of the mescal.

Then empty the contents of 2 fresh passion fruits and half the kiwi fruit (mashed) through the drink. Decorate with the other half of the kiwi fruit (sliced).

Creativity and artistry is key to making this drink come together. The end result should be a glass full of 6 different flavours.

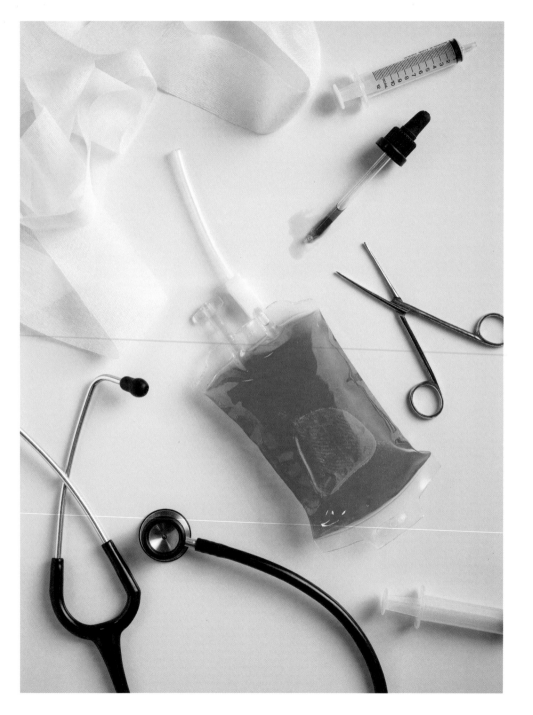

DRIP ADVISOR

The ultimate way to hydrate in summer.

Ingredients

1 sprig fresh lavender

50 ml (2 oz) gin

15 ml (½ oz) violet liqueur

15 ml (½ oz) limoncello

20 ml (¾ oz) elderflower cordial

35 ml (1¼ oz) raspberry cordial or juice

25 ml (1 oz) fresh lemon juice

15 ml (½ oz) lemon thyme syrup ❶

Prep

❶ Add 5 sprigs of fresh lemon thyme to 250 ml (8½ oz) of hot sugar syrup (see page 20). Leave to infuse for at least 4 hours before serving. Remove the thyme after 1 day. It will last for 1 week and makes 15 drinks.

Serve

Add the lavender to a drip bag, if using, or highball. Mix the rest of the ingredients in a mixing jar with ice until sufficiently chilled and diluted before pouring carefully into a drip bag, using a funnel, or highball.

Doctor's Orders:
weight loss, heart health, brain power

Vitamins & Minerals:
vitamin C, antioxidant

Style/Tasting Notes:
floral, aromatic, tart and fruit-driven

Glass/Vessel:
drip bag or high ball

Perfect Serve:
Yerburgh's Jam Jar Gin, Briottet Violette, Pococello Limoncello

PREP 4 HOURS AHEAD

R-2-BEETROOT

You'll feel far from robotic after a sip of this.

Doctor's Orders:
glow

Vitamins & Minerals:
vitamin C, iron, folate, nitrates, potassium

Style/Tasting Notes:
earthy, sweet and savoury

Glass/Vessel:
flamenco highball

Ingredients

50 ml (2 oz) vodka

15 ml (½ oz) dill and fennel shrub ❶

20 ml (¾ oz) shop-bought beetroot juice or golden beetroot purée ❷

20 ml (¾ oz) vanilla syrup ❸

25 ml (1 oz) fresh lemon juice

tonic water, to top

Prep

❶ Slice 2 large bulbs of fennel and add to a storage jar alongside 1 bunch of fresh dill. Pour over 800 ml (28 oz) of base shrub mix (see page 20). Leave at least 1 week before serving. The shrub will keep for 3–6 months and makes 54 drinks.

❷ If making teh purée, peel and boil 6 golden beetroots until soft, then blend with 50 ml (1¾ oz) of the beetroot-flavoured cooking water and 50 ml (1¾ oz) of sugar syrup (see page 24). Blend until smooth and loose, adding more water if necessary.

❸ If making the vanilla syrup, add 1 split vanilla pod to 1 litre (35 oz) of hot sugar syrup (see page 24). Shake regularly and leave for 1 day. The syrup will keep for 1 week in the fridge and makes 25 drinks.

Serve

Add all the ingredients, except the tonic water, to a shaker filled with ice. Shake hard, and then strain into a flamenco highball filled with ice.

PREP
1 WEEK
AHEAD

Garnish

Candied beetroot slices;
beetroot crisps; beetroot
leather (if desired)

To finish it like we do in the
bar, garnish the drink with
candied beetroot slices (slice
candied beetroot thinly
on a mandolin) dispersed
through the glass and store-
bought beetroot crisps.

COMFORTERS

Comfort drinks fall under different guises. They can be luxurious, glutinous, naughty and soothing. Think indulgent dessert cocktails, warming winter toddies and calming under-the-weather drinks. These cocktails are designed to perk you up when you're feeling low.

This chapter hits all the feel-good notes, just don't worry about the calories.

Doctor's Orders:
vascular tone, bone strength

Vitamins & Minerals:
calcium

Style/Tasting Notes:
coconut, grapefruit, chocolate, vanilla, cream, truffle

Glass/Vessel:
mini milk bottle or highball

Perfect Serve:
Hoxton Gin, Bitter Bastards Black Truffle Bitters

WONKA BAR

willy wonka's go to drink

Ingredients

50 ml (1¾ oz) gin

130 ml (4½ oz) almond milk

1 scoop of good quality vanilla ice cream

2 heaped bar spoons of chocolate Oreo soil ❶

5 drops truffle bitters

1 drop truffle oil

Prep

❶ Preheat oven to 60°C (150°F/Gas 0). Blend 1 pack of classic Oreo cookies with 100 grams (3½ oz) of unsalted butter. Lay out the mixture thinly on a baking tray and bake until dry, about 3 hours. Alternatively, dehydrate using a dehydrating tray for 4 hours on a medium temperature until dry.

Serve

Add all the ingredients to a shaker with ice. Shake hard and single strain into mini milk bottle, if using, or highball. Add chipped ice to fill to the neck of the bottle. Place the milk top on the bottle.

PREP
3 HOURS
AHEAD

Doctor's Note

To present this drink like we do at the bar, surround the bottle with chocolate soil, gold leaf and thinly sliced black truffle.

Garnish

Blowtorched fresh sugar cane (if desired)

If desired, use a blowtorch to give the sugar cane colour all over the flesh.

CITIZEN CANE

A double-barrelled rum old-fashioned with a treacle hit.

Ingredients

30 ml (1 oz) aged rum

25 ml (1 oz) agricole rum

½ teaspoon liquid smoke or 10 ml (⅓ oz) smoked sugar syrup ❶

3 drops Angostura bitters

3 drops orange bitters

pink grapefruit peel

Prep

❶ If making the smoked sugar syrup, add 1 bar spoon of smoke powder to 1 litre (35 oz) of hot sugar syrup (see page 24) in a storage jar. Stir the mixture until the powder has dissolved. Alternatively, use a smoking gun (we recommend a Super Aladin Smoker and Aromatizer) with hay or hickory (we like hay) to infuse a jar filled with 1 litre (35 oz) of sugar syrup. Capture the smoke by closing the jar. Repeat the process should you want more smoke but one hit should be enough.

Serve

Add all the ingredients apart from the pink grapefruit to a stirring glass filled with ice. Stir until the mix is sufficiently chilled and strain over chipped ice. Twist pink grapefruit peel over the drink, rim the glass with the peel.

Doctor's Orders:
sugar levels, sleep aid, comforting

Vitamins & Minerals:
fibre

Style/Tasting Notes:
sweet meets raw rum, smooth and sexy

Glass/Vessel:
crystal rocks

Perfect Serve:
Atlantico Private Cask Rum, St. George Agricole Rum, Fee Brothers Orange Bitters

INSTANT CURE

THE ACCIDENTAL TOURIST

Welcome to Miami!

cure for the
holiday blues

Vitamins & Minerals:
vitamins D and C,
antioxidant

Style/Tasting Notes:
half pina çolada, half
frozen raspberry
margarita

Glass/Vessel:
450-ml (16-oz) takeaway
plastic cup with dome
or highball

Perfect Serve:
Ocho Blanco Tequila,
Boiron Raspberry Purée,
El Dorado 3-Year Rum

Ingredients

For the raspberry margarita:

40 ml (1½ oz) blanco tequila

15 ml (½ oz) raspberry purée

4 fresh raspberries

25 ml (1 oz) fresh lime juice

10 ml (⅓ oz) sugar syrup (see page 24)

For the pina colada:

40 ml (1½ oz) rum

50 ml (1¾ oz) fresh or store-bought high-quality pineapple juice, (not from concentrate)

25 ml (1 oz) coconut purée (or coconut milk will do)

Serve

Take all of the raspberry margarita ingredients and add to a bar blender along with 2–3 ice cubes. Blend until the mix is of a slushy consistency. Add another 1–2 ice cubes if needed, then add the mix to the bottom of the plastic cup. Wash out the blender and add the pina çolada ingredients with 2–3 ice cubes and blend until smooth. Take the plastic cup with the original mix and tilt sideways, then pour in the pina çolada mix layering the drink. Fit the cup's dome.

Warning: brain freeze will occur if drunk too fast.

INSTANT
CURE

Garnish
Freeze-dried pineapple,
fresh raspberries (if
desired)

Garnish
Slice of coconut or coconut crisp
(if desired)

Doctor's Note
To present this cocktail the way it was
originally intended, slice open the top of a
coconut and blowtorch the rim before taking
some sand paper and sanding it down. At the
bar, we serve this on a mini BBQ.

COCONUT OLD-FASHIONED

Take an old-fashioned tropical escape.

Doctor's Orders:
take a holiday, hangover cure

Vitamins & Minerals:
potassium

Style/Tasting Notes:
sweet and smoky old-fashioned

Glass/Vessel:
hairy coconut or rocks glass

Perfect Serve:
Ron Millonario Sistema Solera 15-year Rum

Ingredients

50 ml (1¾ oz) aged rum

10 ml (⅓ oz) coconut water syrup reduction ❶

3 drops hickory Angostura bitters ❷ or ordinary Angostura bitters

orange oil

Prep

❶ Add 250 ml (9 oz) of good-quality coconut water and 75 g (3 oz) of caster sugar to a pan over low heat. Stir until the sugar is dissolved, then let the pan simmer for 10–15 minutes until the mix has reduced slightly. Let it cool before pouring into a bottle for serving. The syrup will last for 1 week in the fridge and makes 25 drinks.

❷ If making the hickory Angostura bitters, add 25 ml (1 oz) of Stubb's Hickory Liquid Smoke to 100 ml (3½ oz) of Angostura bitters and pour carefully into a dropper or bitters bottle.

Serve

Add all the ingredients apart from the orange oil to a stirring glass filled with ice. Stir until the mix is sufficiently chilled and strain into the coconut, if using, or rocks glass, over chipped ice.

COMFORTERS

85

INSTANT CURE

SEARCHING FOR SUGAR MAN

An indulgent, fruity twist on a whisky sour.

Doctor's Orders:
heart health, immune system boost

Vitamins & Minerals:
vitamin C, sodium

Style/Tasting Notes:
sweet, smoky, sour

Glass/Vessel:
Olympia Champagne coupe

Perfect Serve:
Nikka From the Barrel Whisky

Ingredients

60 ml (2¼ oz) whisky

30 ml (1 oz) fresh or store-bought pineapple juice (not from concentrate)

25 ml (1 oz) smoked maple syrup ❶ or ordinary maple syrup

25 ml (1 oz) fresh lemon juice

3 drops of Angostura bitters

1 egg white

Prep

❶ Add 1 bar spoon of smoke powder to 1 litre (35 oz) of hot sugar syrup (see page 24) in a storage jar. Stir the mixture until the powder has dissolved. Alternatively, use a smoking gun (we recommend a Super Aladin Smoker and Aromatizer) with hay or hickory (we like hay) to infuse a jar filled with 1 litre (35 oz) of sugar syrup. Capture the smoke by closing the jar. Repeat the process should you want more smoke, but one hit should be enough.

Serve

Add all the ingredients to a shaker. Shake the mix, and then add lots of ice and shake hard. Double strain the mix into an Olympia Champagne coupe.

INSTANT CURE

Garnish
Griddled pineapple slice, grated nutmeg (if desired)

Doctor's Note

To present this drink like we do at the bar, with a pipette dropper, paint 2 lines of vodka on the table next to the glass. Please note, this should be a wooden surface. With obvious caution, light both vodka lines to create Back to the Future fire trails leading to the drink.

In Back to the Future, the Delorean needed to accelerate to 88 mph to time travel. Balkan 176° Vodka has an ABV of 88%. Geeky or what?

Garnish
Lemon peel (if desired)

To garnish, slice a rectangle lemon peel and place on the rim of the glass.

SAZERAC TO THE FUTURE PT 1

A boozy twist on a classic Sazerac which will hurtle you into the future.

Ingredients

50 ml (2 oz) rye whisky

10 ml (⅓ oz) Armagnac

10 ml (⅓ oz) sugar syrup (see page 24)

3 drops Peychaud's Aromatic Bitters or base bitters

2 barspoons Salts of the Earth yellow belly bitters ❶ or 12 ml (¼ oz) Yellow Chartreuse and a pinch of sea salt

Prep

❶ If making Salts of the Earth yellow belly bitters, add 100 ml (3½ oz) of vodka, 50 ml (1¾ oz) of base bitters (see page 22) and 100 ml (3½ oz) of Yellow Chartreuse to a pan with 25 g (1 oz) of chicken salt. Bring the mixture to a simmer to dissolve the salt, then take the mixture off the heat immediately. Pour the mixture once cooled into a bottle.

Serve

Stir all the ingredients in a stirring glass filled with ice until mixed and suitably chilled. Single strain into a frozen Nick and Nora glass. Twist lemon peel over the glass, and rim the glass with another lemon peel.

Doctor's Orders:
brings back memories

Vitamins & Minerals:
salt

Style/Tasting Notes:
a hint of Yellow Chartreuse and saltiness

Glass/Vessel:
Nick and Nora

Perfect Serve:
Rittenhouse 100 Proof Rye Whisky, Bar de Sigognac 10-Year Armagnac, Balkan 176° Vodka

COMFORTERS

INSTANT CURE

REVIVERS

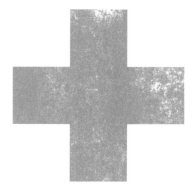

This chapter centres on drinks that can revive and awaken you at any time of day or night. The most famous reviver cocktail, The Corpse Reviver, was first heard of in 1861 and published as a recipe in 1903. The Corpse Reviver (cognac based) and Corpse Reviver #2 (gin based) were made infamous by Harry Craddock in *The Savoy Cocktail Book* (1930). Countless incarnations have been created since then.

Most reviver drinks have a booze-heavy base, elevated further with overproof or high ABV mixers such as absinthe or Chartreuse. The cocktails in this section also fall under martini or Manhattan-style drinks that will perk you up, and tiki-style drinks that pack a punch.

LAST WORDS

Famous for a reason...

Doctor's Orders:
immune system boost, cleanse, aphrodisiac

Vitamins & Minerals:
vitamin C

Style/Tasting Notes:
sweet, sour, herbal, punchy

Glass/Vessel:
vintage coupe

Perfect Serve:
No. 3 London Dry Gin

Ingredients
30 ml (1 oz) dry gin

20 ml (¾ oz) fresh lime juice

15 ml (½ oz) elderflower cordial

10 ml (⅓ oz) Maraschino

10 ml (⅓ oz) Green Chartreuse

10 ml (⅓ oz) Yellow Chartreuse

15 ml (½ oz) fresh pink grapefruit juice

Serve
Add all the ingredients to a shaker filled with ice. Shake hard then double strain into a vintage coupe.

INSTANT CURE

Garnish
Lime twist (if desired)

Garnish

Oregano sea salt rim (if desired)

To make the oregano sea salt rim, muddle together 100 g (3½ oz) of coarse rock salt with 50 g (1¾ oz) dried oregano. Add 25 ml (1 oz) of agave syrup into a cup. Using a small artist's paintbrush, rim half of the Atlantic coupe with the syrup. Then roll that half of the rim in the oregano sea salt mixture and shake off any excess.

Doctor's Note

To present this drink like we do at the bar, top the glass with a bamboo skewer of young feta cheese, black Calamata olive, fresh watermelon and Greek basil. Then serve with side plate of more young feta and mixed olives.

GET HIM TO THE GREEK

A watermelon Martini reinvented with a Greek salad twist, which will bring you back holiday memories.

Doctor's Orders:
cleanse, hydrate

Vitamins & Minerals:
vitamins A, B6 and C, potassium, lycopene, antioxidant

Style/Tasting Notes:
refreshing watermelon, aniseed and herbal hit from the ouzo and bitters

Glass/Vessel:
Champagne coupe

Perfect Serve:
AquaRiva Blanco Tequila

Ingredients

50 ml (1¾ oz) blanco tequila

6.5 ml (¼ oz) ouzo

5 ml (⅕ oz) Salts of the Earth Greek tincture ❶

25 ml (1 oz) fresh watermelon juice

20 ml (¾ oz) fresh lemon juice

20 ml (¾ oz) sugar syrup (see page 24)

Prep

❶ Pour 300 ml (10½ oz) of Skinos Mastiha liqueur (a medicinal/menthol Greek spirit with juniper and spearmint) and 100 ml (3½ oz) of vodka into a Kilner jar. Add 6 Calamata black olives, 6 green Nocellara olives, 1 tablespoon of dried oregano, half a chopped cucumber and 6 stalks of fresh oregano leaves. Leave for at least 2 days to infuse.

Serve

Add all the ingredients to a shaker filled with ice. Shake and then double strain into the glass.

PREP 2 DAYS AHEAD

Doctor's Orders:
protection against silver

Vitamins & Minerals:
vitamins C and K, iron, manganese

Style/Tasting Notes:
a twist on the silver bullet, medicinal, herbaceous, spicy

Glass/Vessel:
martini glass

Perfect Serve:
Portobello Road Dry Gin

WEREWOLF OF LONDON

This delicious concoction will leave you howling for more.

Ingredients
40 ml (1½ oz) dry gin

10 ml (⅓ oz) Maraschino

10 ml (⅓ oz) Wolfschmidt Kummel or Yellow Chartreuse

15 ml (½ oz) juniper and black pepper shrub **❶**

25 ml (1 oz) fresh lemon juice

15 ml (½ oz) sugar syrup (see page 24)

Prep
❶ In a pestle and mortar, muddle 25 crushed fresh juniper berries, 25 crushed black peppercorns and 20 caraway seeds. Add the crushed mixture into 900 ml (32 oz) of white wine base stock shrub (see page 20). Leave for 2 days to infuse. The shrub will last for 3–6 months and makes 60 drinks.

Serve
Shake all the ingredients in a shaker with ice. Double strain the mixture into a Schott Zwiesel Basic Bar Cocktail Glass, or another martini glass, twist grapefruit peel over the glass, and rim the glass with the peel.

PREP
2 DAYS
AHEAD

Garnish

Pink grapefruit werewolf on a mini peg, maraschino cherry, silver sugar tongs (if desired)

If desired, clip a cut-out pink grapefruit werewolf to the rim of the glass and drop the Maraschino cherry into the bottom of the drink. Add silver sugar tongs to the glass (for eating the cherry).

Garnish

Blowtorched fennel slice with fennel frond (if desired)

To make blowtorched fennel, put sliced fennel in iced water with
lemon slices to keep crisp. Take a slice out of the water,
brush with lime and sprinkle with sea salt and cracked pepper. Then,
on a stone or metal surface, torch both sides of the fennel until
charred evenly.

THE SHRUB & SHUTTER

Our signature serve, named after our first bar; an herbal and vegetal twist on a Last Word.

Ingredients

40 ml (1½ oz) gin

20 ml (¾ oz) Green Chartreuse

10 ml (⅓ oz) Maraschino

20 ml (¾ oz) cucumber shrub ❶ or pickle brine

20 ml (¾ oz) toasted fennel seed syrup ❷

20 ml (¾ oz) fresh lime juice

4 drops Salts of the Earth chlorophyll tincture ❸

Prep

❶ If making the shrub, blend 2 large, peeled cucumbers (keep the peel). Add mixture to 800 ml (28 oz) of stock shrub (see page 20) using half cider vinegar and half white wine vinegar. Leave for 1 day, then strain through a muslin. The shrub will keep for 3–6 months and make 40 drinks.

❷ Toast 2 large heaped tablespoons of fennel seeds in a pan. Add toasted seeds to 400 ml (14 oz) of hot sugar syrup (see page 24). Leave to infuse in a jar with 1 whole fresh fennel bulb for 2 days. The syrup will keep for 3–6 months.

❸ Add ½ bunch each of dill, coriander (cilantro), tarragon, flat leaf parsley, Thai basil and the peeled trimmings from cucumber shrub (above) to a large jar. Pour in 500 ml (17½ oz) of vodka and 500 ml (17½ oz) of gin. Leave for 1 day, then remove all the herbs.

Serve

Shake all the ingredients in a shaker with ice. Double strain into a wine glass. Then twist lime peel over the rim and into the drink.

Doctor's Orders:
skincare, metabolism, cleanse, digestion

Vitamins & Minerals:
vitamin C, potassium

Style/Tasting Notes:
herbaceous, aniseed notes

Glass/Vessel:
fancy wine glass

Perfect Serve:
Whitley Neill Dry Gin

PREP 2 DAYS AHEAD

energy, against doctor's orders

Vitamins & Minerals:
vitamins C, B1 and B6, manganese, iron, calcium

Style/Tasting Notes:
tropical, nutty, spicy, sweet and sour

Glass/Vessel:
vintage tankard

Perfect Serve:
El Dorado 3-Year White Rum, El Dorado 8-Year Golden Rum, Myers Dark Rum

AVER ZOMBIE & BITCH

Watch out, this monstrous potion can be a truth serum.

Ingredients

25 ml (1 oz) white rum

20 ml (¾ oz) golden rum

15 ml (½ oz) dark rum

25 ml (1 oz) passion fruit purée

50 ml (1¾ oz) fresh or store-bought pineapple juice (not from concentrate)

½ teaspoon sesame oil

20 ml (¾ oz) grenadine

20 ml (¾ oz) fresh lime juice

10 ml (⅓ oz) pomegranate shrub ❶ or strawberry vinegar

Prep

❶ If making the shrub, using gloves to avoid stains, deseed/bang out 2 fresh pomegranates into a large Kilner jar. Add 100 ml (3½ oz) of grenadine, 200 ml (7 oz) of pomegranate juice and cover with 800 ml (28 oz) of stock shrub (see page 20) using equal parts red wine vinegar and cider vinegar. Leave for at least 2 days. The shrub will last 3–6 months and makes 40 drinks.

Serve

Add all the ingredients to a shaker filled with ice. Then hard shake and single strain over the ice-filled vintage tankard.

PREP 2 DAYS AHEAD

Garnish
½ passion fruit, chargrilled or fresh
pineapple, fresh cherry, fresh mint
sprig (if desired)

Doctor's Note
You don't have to set the passion fruit on fire, but
it's more fun. Add cinnamon powder to a salt shaker and
then douse the passion fruit with vodka and light it, shake
the powder over the flame to send sparks flying.

Doctor's Note

To serve it like we do in the bar, garnish with cured smoked salmon on a skewer. Dress the salmon with mixed baby cress and a grind of black pepper. Our favorite is St. George Terroir Gin-cured smoked salmon (supplied by our friend James Eagle of The Pished Fish – www.thepishedfish.com)

DOES A BEAR SHIT IN THE WOODS?

This drink was inspired by the idea of bears hunting salmon in the Californian wilderness.

Ingredients

35 ml (1¼ oz) gin

15 ml (½ oz) dild akvavit or ordinary akvavit infused with fresh dill

10 ml (⅓ oz) Cocchi Americano

10 ml (⅓ oz) sugar

5 ml (⅕ oz) Salts of the Earth Douglas pine and bay leaf tincture ❶

Prep

❶ Add 200 g (7 oz) of fresh Douglas fir needles and 4 fresh bay leaves to 200 ml (7 oz) of gin and 200 ml (7 oz) of vodka in a large Kilner jar and leave for at least 2 days. Then strain using a sieve to remove the pine needles.

Serve

Add all the ingredients into a mixing jar filled with ice. Stir until mixed and sufficiently chilled. Single strain into a frozen Nick and Nora martini glass.

Doctor's Orders:
lowers stress, good for joints

Vitamins & Minerals:
vitamins B12 and D

Style/Tasting Notes:
forest, pine, gin-cured fresh fish

Glass/Vessel:
Nick and Nora

Perfect Serve:
St. George Terroir Gin, Balkan 176° Vodka

PREP
2 DAYS
AHEAD

LIDO SOUR

Like diving into an azure swimming pool.

Vitamins & Minerals:
vitamins C and D

Style/Tasting Notes:
super refreshing margarita, zesty orange, orange Tic Tac

Glass/Vessel:
crystal rocks

Perfect Serve:
Ocho Blanco Tequila, Solerno Blood Orange Liqueur

Ingredients

20 ml (¾ oz) agave syrup

50 ml (2 oz) tequila

10 ml (⅓ oz) blue curaçao

10 ml (⅓ oz) blood orange liqueur or Cointreau

25 ml (1 oz) fresh lime juice

Serve

Add all the ingredients into a shaker filled with ice and shake hard. Single strain to the glass over chipped ice.

INSTANT CURE

Garnish

Salt and citric acid rim,
swimmers (if desired)

To make the salt rim, add 250 g
(9 oz) of sea salt and 50 g (2 oz)
of citric acid together to form
the rim mixture. Store in a dry
container for serving. If you
don't have citric acid, simply rim
with the sea salt.

Take the glass and, with a small
brush, paint agave syrup around
half of the rim. Then dip the
brushed edge of the glass into
the salt and citric acid rim mix.
Shake off any excess.

Garnish
Thyme sprigs (if desired)

Doctor's Note
At the bar we garnish this cocktail with Chartreuse jelly ❶ and gin-coated gummy bears ❷:

❶ If making the Chartreuse jelly, line a small, shallow oven tray (approximately 30 cm (12 in) by 15 cm (6 in)) with 2 layers of cling film (plaastic wrap). Make sure the cling film goes into the corners to allow liquid to fill the whole tray. Next, add 150 ml (5¼ oz) of Green Chartreuse, 150 ml (5¼ oz) of Yellow Chartreuse, 75 ml (2¾ oz) of lemon juice and 75 ml (2¾ oz) of sugar syrup to a pan, making 450 ml (16 oz) of liquid. Bring this to a simmer on a low heat.

Soak 5 gelatine leaves in a bowl of cold water until floppy. Squeeze the leaves to get rid of excess water. Then add the gelatine to the simmering pan. Stir with a whisk until the gelatine has dissolved. Strain the liquid into the lined tray. Put into the fridge to set for 30–45 minutes. Once set, cut cubes of jelly to your desired shape, using a sharp knife.

❷ If making the gin-coated gummy bears, add 25 ml (1 oz) of dry gin to a small bowl. Brush the store-bought gummy bears until lightly coated with the gin.

YOU CAN'T HANDLE CHARTREUSE!

#truthserum

A celebration of the monk's favourite liqueur.

Ingredients

40 ml (1½ oz) dry gin

10 ml (⅓ oz) mescal

10 ml (⅓ oz) Yellow Chartreuse

5 ml (⅕ oz) Green Chartreuse

25 ml (1 oz) elderflower cordial

20 ml (¾ oz) fresh lemon juice

50 ml (1¾ oz) fresh or store-bought pineapple juice (not from concentrate)

Serve

Shake all the ingredients in a shaker with ice then pour all the contents of the shaker into the jelly mould. Top with ice until bountiful.

Doctor's Orders:
digestion, medical slap in the face

Vitamins & Minerals:
vitamin C, fibre

Style/Tasting Notes:
smoky, sweet and sharp, a long boozy gin sour

Glass/Vessel:
500 ml (17½ oz) glass jelly mould

REVIVERS

INSTANT CURE

Doctor's Orders:
comfort, warmth

Vitamins & Minerals:
protein, amino acids, enzymes

Style/Tasting Notes:
smoky, woody cigar-infused old-fashioned

Glass/Vessel:
vintage crystal brandy balloon

Perfect Serve:
Eagle Rare 10-Year Bourbon, Capovilla Tabacco Leaf Grappa, Fee Brothers Orange Bitters, Weleda Birch Juice

DEER HUNTER

A highlander & hunted old fashioned.

Ingredients

50 ml (1¾ oz) American whisky

10 ml (⅓ oz) grappa

5 ml (⅕ oz) Salts of the Earth cigar bitters ❶

7.5 ml (¼ oz) sugar syrup

5 ml (⅕ oz) Birch juice

3 drops of Angostura bitters

2 drops of orange bitters

orange peel

dill

Prep

❶ Add 100 ml (3½ oz) of Grappa to 100 ml (3½ oz) of base bitters (see page 22). Add 2 Cuban cigars (your preference) and leave to infuse for at least 2 weeks.

Serve

Add all the ingredients to a mixing glass with ice. Stir until sufficiently chilled. Single strain into the vintage crystal brandy balloon over chipped ice. Then twist an orange peel over the drink.

PREP
2 WEEKS
AHEAD

Garnish
orange peel; dill (if desired)

Doctor's Note
At the bar we serve this drink with venison carpaccio rolled in dill with pistachio crumb and fresh thyme. If you'd like to do so as well:

Take a venison loin and, with a sharp knife, remove any sinew. Slice the loin into long 5-cm (2-inch) cylinders. Then finely chop a large sprig of dill and sprinkle all over the venison. Season with salt and black pepper. Wrap each piece of meat tightly in cling film (plastic wrap) to make a sausage shape, then twist the ends of the cling film to tighten the roll. Put the venison in a fridge to firm up. After 1 hour remove the meat from the fridge to be sliced for serving.

Using a pestle and mortar, break pistachio nuts into a crumb. Slice the venison thinly with a sharp knife. Sprinkle each slice with pistachio crumb and another touch of sea salt and cracked pepper. Pierce 1 slice of venison per drink with a bamboo skewer then garnish the top of the drink.

CHERRY POPPER

It might be your first time with this drink, but it won't be your last.

Ingredients

40 ml (1½ oz) aged bourbon infused with fresh cherry ❶

15 ml (½ oz) sweet vermouth

10 ml (⅓ oz) Maraschino

3 drops cherry bitters (see page 23)

orange peel

Prep

❶ Slice 12 fresh cherries and add to a storage jar with a 700 ml (18½ oz) bottle of aged bourbon. Leave to infuse for at least 2 days before straining. Keep cherries for special cocktails (muddling) or garnishing drinks. This will make enough for 14 drinks.

Serve

Stir all the ingredients in a stirring glass with ice until chilled before straining into a frozen Nick and Nora glass. Twist the orange peel over the drink before rimming the glass with the peel.

Garnish

Fresh, chilled cherry on rim (if desired)

Doctor's Orders:
repair cells, warmth

Vitamins & Minerals:
antioxidant

Style/Tasting Notes:
a sweet smooth Manhattan, cherry flavours

Glass/Vessel:
Nick and Nora

Perfect Serve:
Smooth Ambler Old Scout Bourbon, Antica Formula Carpano Vermouth, Luxardo Maraschino

REVIVERS

PREP 2 DAYS AHEAD

FIRST AID BOX

For use in any emergency.

Doctor's Orders:
energy, antiseptic, cold clearer

Vitamins & Minerals:
potassium, niacin, magnesium, vitamin E, calcium, zinc

Style/Tasting Notes:
marzipan, vanilla, flowery smoke, liquorice flavours

Glass/Vessel:
first-aid box takeaway cup

Perfect Serve:
Patrón XO Cafe Tequila, Ron Atlantico Private Cask Rum

Ingredients
25 ml (1 oz) vanilla-infused white rum ❶ or use vanilla-flavoured rum

25 ml (1 oz) coffee-flavoured tequila

50 ml (2 oz) espresso

20 ml (¾ oz) white chocolate syrup or chocolate sauce

50 ml (2 oz) soy milk

Prep
❶ If making the infused rum, add 1 split vanilla pod to a 700 ml (18½ oz) bottle of white rum. Leave to infuse for 1 day, shaking regularly. It will make enough for 14 drinks.

Serve
Add all the ingredients to a shaker filled with ice. Shake very hard then single strain into a takeaway cup with no ice.

PREP
1 DAY
AHEAD

Doctor's Note
At the bar we serve this drink with a coffee mousse, served in a petri dish. You don't have to do it, but you should.

Garnish
Grated tonka bean (if desired)

Garnish

Grapefruit peel, strawberry candy
laces (if desired)

To make the grapefruit peel parcels,
wrap a strawberry lace tightly
around a fresh pink grapefruit peel,
and add it to the drink.

Doctor's Note

At the bar we create the drink at the table (multiply
the ingredients by 10 and serve in a 3-part stacking
bottle). The whole bottle and the glasses are to be
served in a travelling trunk or briefcase smoked with
straw (using a smoking gun or blowtorch).

STRAW MAN PROPOSAL

An interactive sharing negroni
to cure a crowd.

Ingredients

25 ml (9 oz) dry gin

25 ml (9 oz) Campari

25 ml (9 oz) sweet vermouth

25 ml (4½ oz) strawberry
vermouth

Serve

Single strain the chilled mixture into a timeless rocks
glass over chipped ice. Twist a pink grapefruit peel
over the drink and then rim the glass with the peel.

Doctor's Orders:
decision-making

Vitamins & Minerals:
vitamin C, magnesium,
potassium, manganese,
antioxidant

Style/Tasting Notes:
strawberry-flavoured
negroni; the bitterness
is softened by the
strawberry vermouth

Glass/Vessel:
timeless rocks

Perfect Serve:
Whitley Neill
Handcrafted Dry
Gin, Mancino
Vermouth Rosso
(or Martini Rosso),
Dolin Chamberyzette
Strawberry Aperitif

INSTANT
CURE

Doctor's Orders:
cleanse, cold cure

Vitamins & Minerals:
vitamin C, antioxidant

Style/Tasting Notes:
spicy, floral, sweet and sour

Glass/Vessel:
Olympia Champagne coupe

Perfect Serve:
Ocho Blanco Tequila, Briottet Coquelicot de Nemours (Poppy) Liqueur, Boiron Apricot Purée

MISSION IMPOSSIBLE

See out the night with a bang.

Ingredients
45 ml (1½ oz) blanco tequila

10 ml (⅓ oz) poppy liqueur

10 ml (⅓ oz) fresh cloudy apple juice

12.5 ml (½ oz) ginger and lemongrass cordial

10 ml (⅓ oz) apricot purée

15 ml (½ oz) fresh lemon juice

4 drops of rose water

pink grapefruit peel

Serve
Add all the ingredients to a shaker full of ice, shake hard, and double strain into an Olympia Champagne coupe. To garnish, twist a pink grapefruit peel over the top of the glass.

INSTANT CURE

Garnish

Lemon popping candy rim (if desired)

For the candy rim, take the glass and, with a small brush, paint agave syrup around half of the rim. Then dip the brushed edge of the glass into lemon popping candy. Shake off any excess.

Doctor's Note

There's no need to set this on fire if you're really attached to your eyebrows. But if you're feeling brave, then tie the flash string around the stem of the glass, attaching the cotton wool underneath the stem. Once at the table, roll out the string and ignite.

Garnish

Orange peel cross (if desired)

To create an orange cross, use exemplary knife skills or use a cross-shaped cookie cutter.

COFFEE + CIGARETTES

Combine all your vices into one drink.

Doctor's Orders:
energy, smoke hit

Vitamins & Minerals:
potassium, niacin,
magnesium, vitamin E,
calcium, zinc

Style/Tasting Notes:
bittersweet, complex,
layers of flavour

Glass/Vessel:
small Chicago rocks

Ingredients

25 ml (1 oz) Campari

15 ml (½ oz) Picon aperitif à
l'orange

15 ml (½ oz) amaretto

25 ml (1 oz) espresso

2 dashes orange bitters

Serve

Add all the ingredients to a stirring glass filled with
ice. Stir the mix down until sufficiently chilled and
single strain into a chilled frozen small Chicago rocks
glass. Twist orange peel over the drink and rim the
glass with the peel before discarding.

INSTANT
CURE

RESTORE/ RECTIFY

The notion of how to cure a hangover has been debated forever. The hope is that the hair of the dog cocktails included in this chapter will help to ease your pain.

This section has more vegetal and savoury drinks, like The Bloody Mary. The invention of The Bloody Mary has been claimed by many a bartender going back to the 1920s and has been called many things and been made hundreds of ways. The name is supposedly a reference to Queen Mary I of England but some say it was inspired by Mary Pickford a Hollywood actress of yesteryear. The Bloody Mary also falls into the anti-fogmatics category (or cocktails to clear the fog). This category of drink is growing fast and ties in nicely with more healthy drinking and eating.

Doctor's Orders:
hydration, digestion

Vitamins & Minerals:
vitamins A and C,
potassium, calcium

Style/Tasting Notes:
acidic Bloody Mary,
salty and sour

Glass/Vessel:
highball

Perfect Serve:
Pisco El Gobernador

TIGER'S MILK

Ceviche in a drink – it doesn't get fresher than this.

Ingredients

50 ml (2 oz) pisco

30 ml (1 oz) pink grapefruit juice

25 ml (1 oz) fresh lime juice

100 ml (3½ oz) clarified tomato juice ❶ or a good quality tomato juice

¼ red chilli, finely chopped

large pinch sea salt and cracked black pepper

2 drops celery bitters (optional) (see page 23)

2 large pinches coriander (cilantro), 1 for garnish

1 thumb finely chopped ginger (¾ inside the drink ¼ for garnish)

Prep

❶ If making fresh tomato juice, using a juice extractor, juice 5 kg (11 lb) tomatoes. Add 100 ml (3½ oz) of lemon juice and season with salt and pepper to taste. Strain through a muslin and store the juice in the fridge for up to 2 weeks.

Serve

Add all the ingredients except the coriander and ginger to a shaker filled with ice and rock the mix (do not shake). Pour to a highball, with the ice. Add 1 large pinch of coriander and ¾ of the finely chopped ginger to the glass and disperse evenly. Top with ice if needed.

INSTANT CURE

Garnish
Coriander (cilantro) cress or ordinary coriander, fresh ginger, fresh mint sprig (if desired)

Garnish
Iced sea lettuce (or samphire), sea buckthorn curd, dashi jelly (if desired)

Doctor's Note
For theatre, serve on a tea smoker
with seaweed dry-ice essence
(obviously optional).

ROCK POOL

Dive into this spicy, smoky drink.

Ingredients

50 ml (2 oz) dry gin

10 ml (⅓ oz) samphire and rosemary shrub ❶

100 ml (3½ oz) fresh tomato water ❷ or tomato juice

4 drops green tabasco

10 ml (⅓ oz) sea buckthorn juice or fresh orange juice

2 large pinches of sea salt (to taste)

2 grinds cracked black pepper

Method

❶ Take 200 g (7 oz) of washed samphire and 50 g (2 oz) of sea rosemary (or ordinary rosemary) and add to 900 ml (32 oz) of base white wine vinegar shrub (see page 20). Leave for at least 2 days before using.

❷ If making fresh tomato juice, juice 2 kg (70 oz) of plum tomatoes through a juice extractor. Strain the mix through a muslin. Lightly season the juice with 25 ml (1 oz) of fresh lemon juice and 2 pinches of fine table salt.

Serve

Add all the ingredients to a shaker filled with ice then rock the shaker (don't shake) until sufficiently chilled. Single strain the liquid into the serving bowl. Add chipped ice to the top of the glass.

Doctor's Orders:
fresh sea air, minerals, digestion, hangover cure

Vitamins & Minerals:
vitamin C

Style/Tasting Notes:
clean super fresh tomato, acidic and spice

Glass/Vessel:
glass bowl vase

Perfect Serve:
Tarquin's Cornish Dry Gin

PREP
2 DAYS
AHEAD

NAUGHTY PIGLET

A bistro cocktail inspired by our friends at Naughty Piglets.

Doctor's Orders:

healing benefit, heart health, skin health, digestion, brainpower, bone health

Vitamins & Minerals:
vitamins C and K

Style/Tasting Notes:
earthy, mineral, sweet, savoury

Glass/Vessel:
highball

Perfect Serve:
Grey Goose Poire Vodka, Berneroy XO Calvados

Ingredients

40 ml (1½ oz) pear vodka or or ordinary vodka mixed with 10 ml (⅓ oz) pear purée

20 ml (¾ oz) calvados

10 ml (⅓ oz) celeriac shrub ❶

25 ml (1 oz) dry white wine (like a Sancerre)

25 ml (1 oz) Dijon and grain mustard honey syrup ❷

25 ml (1 oz) fresh cloudy apple juice

25 ml (1 oz) fresh lemon juice

Prep

❶ Wash and scrub a small celeriac. Then, with a knife or skewer, puncture 20 holes through the flesh. Next slice the celeriac in half and add to a storage jar. Pour over 800 ml (28 oz) of base cider vinegar shrub (page 20) to submerge. Add a large ball of cling film (plastic wrap) to the top of the jar to push down the celeriac should it float. Leave for at least 2 days (but the longer the better) before using for service. the shrub will keep for 3–6 months and makes 80 drinks.

❷ Put 250 ml (8½ oz) of honey in a pan, and then add 2 tablespoons of Dijon and grain mustards. Pour over 50 ml (2 oz) of boiling water and stir until completely mixed and loosened. Pour the mix into a squeeze bottle for serving.

Serve

Add all the ingredients to a shaker filled with ice and shake hard. Single strain the mix into a highball over ice.

PREP 2 DAYS AHEAD

Garnish
Julienne celeriac sticks, fresh sliced
pear, mustard sour cream (if desired)

Garnish

Fresh herbs and cress (if desired)

LITTLE MISS SUNSHINE

Sunshine in a glass.

Ingredients

50 ml (2 oz) dry gin

100 ml (3½ oz) yellow tomato juice (or ordinary tomato juice for a Little Miss Sunset)

10 ml (⅓ oz) elderflower cordial

5 ml (⅕ oz) balsamic vinegar

20 ml (¾ oz) yuzu dressing

10 ml (⅓ oz) Scotch bonnet house hot sauce ❶ or green Tabasco

2 large pinches sea salt

2 large pinches cracked black pepper

3 drops celery bitters (see page 23)

Prep

❶ If making Scotch bonnet hot sauce, add 1 teaspoon of vegetable oil to a hot pan, follow with 20 mixed deseeded and sliced Scotch bonnet chillies, 6 fresh sliced jalapeño chillies, 1 finely chopped large red onion, 6 cloves of finely chopped garlic, 1 teaspoon of cooking salt, 300 ml (10½ oz) of cold water, 75 ml (2¾ oz) of white wine vinegar, 50 ml (2 oz) of fresh lime juice, 25 ml (1 oz) of tomato purée and 2 large tablespoons of sugar. Then bring the mixture to a gentle simmer, stirring frequently. Wait until all the ingredients are soft, and then cook for a further 20 minutes. Next, in a food processor, blend the mixture until smooth.

Serve

Add all the ingredients to a shaker filled with ice. Gently roll and rock the shaker to mix the drink without diluting the ice. Once chilled, single strain the mixture into an ice-filled crystal highball.

Doctor's Orders:
hangover cure, sunshine glow

Vitamins & Minerals:
vitamins A, B6, C and K, biotin, phosphorus

Style/Tasting Notes:
cleansing, yellow tomato Bloody Mary, sweet and juicy

Glass/Vessel:
crystal highball

Perfect Serve:
Whitley Neill Dry Gin, The Bitter Truth Celery Bitters

INSTANT CURE

JUGGED PEAS

Petit pois à la Francais.

Doctor's Orders:
mender, flu zapper, hangover cure

Vitamins & Minerals:
vitamins A, C, E and K, zinc, fibre, folate

Style/Tasting Notes:
a cleansing chicken and ham soup, fresh mint and spice

Glass/Vessel:
Gisela Graham chicken jug (small jug for a single serve or large for sharing) and highball

Perfect Serve:
Snow Queen Organic Vodka

Ingredients

100 ml (3½ oz) pea-shoot-infused vodka ❶

150 ml (5¼ oz) homemade chicken and ham stock ❷

100 ml (3½ oz) good-quality tomato consommé

50 ml (1¾ oz) fresh lemon juice

3 large pinches of chicken salt

2 large pinches of cracked black pepper

1 handful of fresh pea-shoots

8 fresh mint leaves

6 dashes green Tabasco sauce

Prep

❶ Add a 70 cl bottle of vodka to a large Kilner jar with 4 large handfuls of pea-shoots. Leave the mixture for 1 day then remove the shoots. The vodka should be a vibrant green colour.

❷ Roast 6 chicken legs, 6 chicken wings and 1 medium-sized ham hock in a very large pan with olive oil until golden brown. Then add 2 large pinches of salt, 2 pieces of chicken salt, 2 large grinds of black pepper, 4 cloves of garlic, 4 bay leaves, 2 fresh rosemary sprigs, 2 large chopped onions, 4 large chopped carrots, 6 sticks of celery, 1 tablespoon of fennel seeds, 20 pink peppercorns, 2 star anise, 6 cloves, 1 teaspoon of chilli flakes, 50 ml (1¾ oz) of fresh lemon juice and 100 ml (3½ oz) of cider vinegar. Add 400 ml (14 oz) of white wine and enough water to cover. Leave the pan to simmer for up to 4 hours until the ham and the chicken break down. Every half an hour skim the top. Let the pan cool before straining the liquid off. Season to taste.

PREP
1 DAY
AHEAD

Garnish

Crispy chicken skin ❸, raw asparagus spears, pan-fried crispy bacon, fresh peas, free pea-shoots, fresh mint leaves, fresh mint sprigs (if desired)

❸ Spread chicken skins (free from most good butchers) on a silicone baking mat on a baking tray. Lightly season the skin with chicken salt and cracked black pepper. Place another baking tray over the skins to keep them from puffing. Roast in a 200°C (400°F/ Gas 6) oven for 30 minutes. Turn up the oven to 250°C (485°F/ Gas 9) and cook for another 30 minutes. Remove the skins and dry them off with paper towel. If the skins are still not crisp you can always deep fry for a few more seconds.

Serve

Add the fresh pea-shoots and fresh mint to a big mixing jar then gently muddle. Next, add all the other ingredients and ice to the jar. Stirring until thoroughly mixed and chilled. Double strain into the chicken jug.

Garnish

Flower petals, wild garlic flower, spring onion (scallion), borage flower
(if desired)

TERIYAKI MANHATTAN

Toyko meets Manhattan.

Doctor's Orders:
enhances umami

Vitamins & Minerals:
vitamin B12

Style/Tasting Notes:
creamy, sweet but salty

Glass/Vessel:
wooden noodle bowl

Perfect Serve:
El Dorado 12-Year Aged
Rum, Rittenhouse
Straight Rye 100 Whisky

Ingredients

30 ml (1 oz) aged rum

20 ml (¾ oz) rye whisky

10 ml (⅓ oz) vermouth

10 ml (⅓ oz) house teriyaki dressing ❶ or store-bought teriyaki sauce

10 ml (⅓ oz) sugar syrup (see page 24)

Prep

❶ If making dressing, mix 100 ml (3½ oz) of soy sauce, 50 ml (2 oz) of water, 2 tablespoons of sweet rice wine, 1 tablespoon of honey, 2 tablespoons of brown sugar, 1½ teaspoons of minced fresh garlic and 1½ teaspoons of minced fresh ginger in a saucepan over a low heat. Simmer, stirring, until the sugar has dissolved.

Serve

Stir all the ingredients in a stirring glass with ice until mixed and chilled sufficiently. Single strain into a wooden noodle bowl, if using, or rocks glass, over chipped ice.

INSTANT CURE

Doctor's Orders:
detox, hangover cure, digestion, brain function

Vitamins & Minerals:
vitamins C and K, iron, zinc, potassium, manganese, phosphorus and zinc

Style/Tasting Notes:
dry and bitter whisky-style negroni

Glass/Vessel:
spirits snifter

Perfect Serve:
Nikka From the Barrel Whisky, Akashi-Tai Daiginjo Sake

LOST IN TRANSLATION

Revisiting a classic negroni with Japanese ingredients.

Ingredients
30 ml (1 oz) whisky

15 ml (½ oz) Campari

20 ml (¾ oz) Cynar

10 ml (⅓ oz) sake

5 ml (⅕ oz) sugar syrup (see page 24)

pink grapefruit peel

Serve
Stir all the ingredients in a stirring glass with ice until sufficiently mixed and chilled. Single strain mixture into the spirits snifter. Twist the pink grapefruit peel over the top of the snifter and rim the glass with the peel.

INSTANT CURE

Garnish

Pickled soy girolle mushrooms
(if desired)

To make, clean 100 g (3 ½ oz)
girolle mushrooms with a soft
pastry paintbrush to remove any
dirt. Then add the mushrooms to
pickled soy dressing. To make the
soy dressing, add 100 ml (3½ oz)
of light soy sauce to a jar along
with 100 ml (3½ oz) of mirin,
5 ml (⅕ oz) of fish sauce, 25 ml
(1 oz) of brown sugar syrup, 25 ml
(1 oz) of fresh lime juice, 10 pink
peppercorns and ¼ thumb of
finely chopped fresh ginger.
Stir all the ingredients until
thoroughly mixed.

Doctor's Note

At the bar we like to pair this drink with
a cheese and seed cracker topped with
Montgomery's Mature Cheddar, aged Comté
and quince paste. We like to change the cheese
selection according to the seasons.

THE OWL &
THE PUSSYCAT

A cheese board in a drink – perfect for after dinner.

Ingredients

30 ml (1 oz) gin

10 ml (⅓ oz) quince brandy

15 ml (½ oz) umeshu

10 ml (⅓ oz) Armagnac

4 drops celery bitters (see page 23)

20 ml (¾ oz) quince shrub ❶

25 ml (1 oz) fresh lemon juice

10 ml (⅓ oz) sugar syrup (see page 24)

Prep

❶ Add 200 g (7 oz) of quince paste to 800 ml (28 oz) of cider vinegar base shrub (see page 20) and leave to infuse for 1 day.

Serve

Shake all the ingredients together in a shaker filled with ice. Double strain into a chilled Nick and Nora glass.

Doctor's Orders:
digestion, cholesterol, relaxation

Vitamins & Minerals:
vitamin C, calcium

Style/Tasting Notes:
sweet and boozy martini, with quince, plum and refreshing celery notes

Glass/Vessel:
Nick and Nora

Perfect Serve:
Langley's No. 8 Gin, Akashi-Tai Shiraume Ginjo Umeshu, Baron de Sigognac Bas Armagnac, The Bitter Truth Celery Bitters

RESTORE/RECTIFY

137

PREP
1 DAY
AHEAD

COCKTAIL PARTY IDEAS

Friends over? Then you want to impress.... cocktails can be kept fuss-free and simple, but beautiful. Prep is the key.

Seasonal Drinks

The occasion and time of year will help to dictate what drinks you should be making.

Christmas

eggnogs, snowballs, old fashioneds, mulled wines, toddies

Easter

chocolate martinis, hot cross bun martinis, brandy alexanders, white chocolate pina çoladas

Thanksgiving

pumpkin margaritas, bacon old fashioneds, turkey-infused bloody marys

Fireworks Night/Halloween

corpse revivers, fog cutters, nuclear daiquiris

Spring/Summer

collins, daisies, martini twists

Tips for Cocktail Party Success

It is important to get the drinks right for a party, as you want everyone to have a go-to beverage. To cover all bases you should have one long, one short, one bitter, one sweet. Definitely have beers and bubbly as back ups! If you want to keep it simpler, one long and one short will do. Mojitos and fruit martinis are always crowd pleasers.

Start with less complex drinks so you don't keep your guests waiting – have a simple G&T, spritz or bellini ready at the start of the party so everyone can wet their whistles without delay.

A SIMPLE SPRITZ RECIPE

50 ml (1¾ oz) liqueur – eg. aperol, Campari, vermouth, eau de vie

75 ml (2½ oz) sparkling wine – prosecco or Champagne

25 ml (1 oz) top – soda, tonic

Batching cocktails is always a good way to ensure ease of service, with punches being the obvious choice. A D.I.Y. drinks station always works as well so people can pick and choose what they want.

INDEX

The Accidental Tourist 82–3
agave syrup: Papaya the Sailorman
    60–1
Akashi-Tai Daiginjo: Jiro Dreams of
    Sushi 68–9
akvavit: Does a Bear Shit in the
    Woods? 102–3
almond milk: Wonka Bar 78–9
aloe vera juice: Drugstore Cowboy
    58–9
Amaretto: Coffee + Cigarettes
    118–19
angostura bitters
    Ball Park Figure 42–3
    Coconut Old-Fashioned 84–5
aperitivos 14
An Apple a Day 46–7
apple juice
    An Apple a Day 46–7
    Mission Impossible 116–17
apple shrub: An Apple a Day 46–7
apples
    An Apple a Day 46–7
    celery bitters 23
apricot purée: Mission Impossible
    116–17
armagnac
    The Owl & the Pussycat 136–7
    Sazerac to the Future Pt 1: 88–9
Aver Zombie & Bitch 100–1

Ball Park Figure 42–3
Bandage of Brothers 64–5
bar ingredients 14
base recipes
    base bitter recipe 22
    base tinctures 24
    celery bitters 23

cherry bitters 23
    D.I.Y. bitters 22
    ginger bitters 23
    shrubs 20–1
beeswax: lip balm 67
beetroot
    Beets By Wray 32–3
    R-2-Beetroot 74–5
Beets By Wray 32–3
Bigallet Thym Liqueur: Pollen Count
    52–3
bitters 14
    base bitter recipe 22
    celery bitters 23
    cherry bitters 23
    D.I.Y. bitters 22
    ginger bitters 23
bourbon 13
    Ball Park Figure 42–3
    base tinctures 24
    Cherry Popper 110–11
brandy 13
    The Owl & the Pussycat 136–7
Briottet Violette liqueur: Pollen
    Count 52–3

cachaça: Beets By Wray 32–3
calvados
    An Apple a Day 46–7
    Naughty Piglet 126–7
campari
    Coffee + Cigarettes 118–19
    Lost in Translation 134–5
    Smoke the Weed 36–7
    Strawman Proposal 114–15
Captain Planet 70–1
cardamom bitters: Drugstore Cowboy
    58–9

carrot & celery shrub: Who Framed
    Roger Rabbit? 54–5
celeriac shrub: Naughty Piglet 126–7
celery bitters 23
celery syrup: Who Framed Roger
    Rabbit? 54–5
Chartreuse
    Dr Greenthumb 56–7
    Field Notes 40–1
    Last Words 92–3
    Parklife 48–9
    Sazerac to the Future Pt 1: 88–9
    The Shrub & Shutter 98–9
    Thirst Aid 44–5
    You Can't Handle Chartreuse!
    106–7
cherries
    cherry bitters 23
    Cherry Popper 110–11
cherry brandy: cherry bitters 23
chicken & ham stock: Jugged Peas
    130–1
chilli flakes: Jungle Fever 66–7
chillies: Tiger's Milk 122–3
cider vinegar base shrub 20–1
    An Apple a Day 46–7
    Cucumber Daiquiri 38–9
    ginger & roasted meadow hay
    syrup 54–5
    Pollen Count 52–3
    R+H+U+B+A+R+B 50–1
Citizen Cane 80–1
cocktail parties 138
coconut milk
    Captain Planet 70–1
    Jungle Fever 66–7
coconut oil: lip balm 67
Coconut Old-Fashioned 84–5

coconut purée: The Accidental
    Tourist 82–3
coconut water
    Coconut Old-Fashioned 84–5
    Jungle Fever 66–7
coffee
    Coffee + Cigarettes 118–19
    First Aid Box 112–13
cognac: An Apple a Day 46–7
cordials & syrups 14
Cucumber Daiquiri 38–9
cucumber juice: Dr Greenthumb 56–7
cucumber shrub
    Cucumber Daiquiri 38–9
    The Shrub & Shutter 98–9
curaçao: Lido Sour 104–5
curry paste: Jungle Fever 66–7
Cynar
    Lost in Translation 134–5
    Smoke the Weed 36–7

daiquiri: Cucumber Daiquiri 38–9
dashi: Smoke the Weed 36–7
Deer Hunter 108–9
dill: R-2-Beetroot 74–5
D.I.Y. bitters 22
Does a Bear Shit in the Woods? 102–3
Dolin de Coeur Genepi: Pollen Count
    52–3
Dr Greenthumb 56–7
Dr Seuss 34–5
Drip Advisor 72–3
Drugstore Cowboy 58–9

eau de vies 14
elderflower cordial
    Little Miss Sunshine 128–9
    Parklife 48–9

elderflower liqueur: Parklife 48–9
equipment 16–20
fennel
    R-2-Beetroot 74–5
    The Shrub & Shutter 98–9
Field Notes 40–1
figs
    Ball Park Figure 42–3
    bourbon figs 42
First Aid Box 112–13
fruit: Captain Planet 70–1

garnishing 26
Get Him to the Greek 94–5
gin 12
    base tinctures 24
    cherry bitters 23
    Does a Bear Shit in the Woods?
        102–3
    Dr Greenthumb 56–7
    Dr Seuss 34–5
    Drip Advisor 72–3
    gin-coated gummy bears 106–7
    ginger bitters 23
    Jiro Dreams of Sushi 68–9
    Last Words 92–3
    Little Miss Sunshine 128–9
    The Owl & the Pussycat 136–7
    Parklife 48–9
    R+H+U+B+A+R+B 50–1
    Rock Pool 124–5
    The Shrub & Shutter 98–9
    Strawman Proposal 114–15
    Thirst Aid 44–5
    Watermelon G&T 62–3
    Werewolf of London 96–7
    Who Framed Roger Rabbit?
        54–5

Wonka Bar 78–9
You Can't Handle Chartreuse!
    106–7
ginger
    ginger & roasted meadow hay
        syrup 54–5
    Jungle Fever 66–7
ginger bitters 23
    Ball Park Figure 42–3
    Who Framed Roger Rabbit? 54–5
grappa: Deer Hunter 108–9

honey: lip balm 67

ice cream: Wonka Bar 78–9
infusion: tinctures 24

jelly
    Chartreuse jelly 106–7
    iced sea lettuce, sea buckthorn
        curd, dashi jelly 124–5
    Jiro Dreams of Sushi 68–9
    Jugged Peas 130–1
    Jungle Fever 66–7
juniper berries: Werewolf of London
    96–7

kale crisps 36–7
kiwi fruit: Dr Seuss 34–5

Last Words 92–3
lavender: Pollen Count 52–3
lavender shrub: Pollen Count
    52–3
lemon popping candy rim: Mission
    Impossible 116–17
lemon sherbet: An Apple a Day
    46–7

lemon thyme syrup: Drip Advisor
    72–3
lemongrass essential oil: lip balm 67
Lido Sour 104–5
lime juice: Last Words 92–3
limes: Jungle Fever 66–7
lip balm 67
liqueurs 14
    Spritz 138
liquid smoke: Citizen Cane 80–1
Little Miss Sunshine 128–9
Lost in Translation 134–5

maraschino
    Beets By Wray 32–3
    Cherry Popper 110–11
    Last Words 92–3
    The Shrub & Shutter 98–9
    Werewolf of London 96–7
mescal 13
    Captain Planet 70–1
    Papaya the Sailorman 60–1
    Thirst Aid 44–5
    You Can't Handle Chartreuse!
        106–7
mint
    Dr Greenthumb 56–7
    Drugstore Cowboy 58–9
    Thirst Aid 44–5
miso shrub: Jiro Dreams of Sushi
    68–9
Mission Impossible 116–17
mushrooms
    Field Notes 40–1
    pickled soy girolle mushrooms
        134–5

Naughty Piglet 126–7

Oreo cookies: Wonka Bar 78–9
ouzo: Get Him to the Greek
    94–5
The Owl & the Pussycat 136–7

Papaya the Sailorman 60–1
Parklife 48–9
passion fruit: Aver Zombie & Bitch
    100–1
pear purée: Naughty Piglet 126–7
peas
    Dr Greenthumb 56–7
    Jugged Peas 130–1
peppercorns: Werewolf of London
    96–7
Périgord-blacktruffle-infused whisky:
    Field Notes 40–1
picon aperitif à lorange: Coffee +
    Cigarettes 118–19
pineapple juice
    The Accidental Tourist 82–3
    Aver Zombie & Bitch 100–1
    Searching for Sugar Man 86–7
    Thirst Aid 44–5
    You Can't Handle Chartreuse!
        106–7
pisco: Tiger's Milk 122–3
pistachio nuts: venison carpaccio
    108–9
Pollen Count 52–3
pomegranate shrub: Aver Zombie &
    Bitch 100–1
poppy liqueur
    Bandage of Brothers 64–5
    Mission Impossible 116–17

quince shrub: The Owl & the Pussy-
    cat 136–7

R-2-Beetroot 74–5
raspberries: The Accidental Tourist 82–3
raspberry cordial: Drip Advisor 72–3
R+H+U+B+A+R+B 50–1
rhubarb bitters
    R+H+U+B+A+R+B 50–1
    Watermelon G&T 62–3
rice vinegar: Jiro Dreams of Sushi 68–9
rims
    lemon popping candy rim 116–17
    salt and citric acid rim 104–5
    spiced rim mixture 60–1
Rock Pool 124–5
rum 12
    The Accidental Tourist 82–3
    Aver Zombie & Bitch 100–1
    base tinctures 24
    Beets By Wray 32–3
    Captain Planet 70–1
    Citizen Cane 80–1
    Coconut Old-Fashioned 84–5
    Cucumber Daiquiri 38–9
    Drugstore Cowboy 58–9
    First Aid Box 112–13
    ginger bitters 23
    Jungle Fever 66–7
    Papaya the Sailorman 60–1
    Teriyaki Manhattan 132–3
rye 13
    base tinctures 24

sage: Thirst Aid 44–5
sake: Lost in Translation 134–5
salt and citric acid rim: Lido Sour 104–5

Salts of the Earth chlorophyll tincture 98–9
Salts of the Earth cigar bitters: Deer Hunter 108–9
Salts of the Earth Douglas pine and bayleaf tincture: Does a Bear Shit in the Woods? 102–3
Salts of the Earth Electric Avenue tincture: An Apple a Day 46–7
Salts of the Earth Greek tincture: Get Him to the Greek 94–5
Salts of the Earth yellow belly bitters: Sazerac to the Future Pt 1: 88–9
samphire & rosemary shrub: Rock Pool 124–5
Sazerac to the Future Pt 1: 88–9
Scotch bonnet hot sauce: Little Miss Sunshine 128–9
Scotch, single malt 12
sea buckthorn juice: Rock Pool 124–5
Searching for Sugar Man 86–7
seaweed: Smoke the Weed 36–7
shaking 26
sherbet: beetroot sherbet 32–3
The Shrub & Shutter 98–9
shrubs
    cider vinegar base shrub 20–1
    white wine vinegar base shrub 20–1
Smoke the Weed 36–7
spiced rim mixture: Papaya the Sailorman 60–1
spirits 12–13
Spritz 138
star fruit: Drugstore Cowboy 58–9
stirring 26
strawberry & thyme juice: Dr Seuss 34–5

Strawman Proposal 114–15
sugar syrup 24
suze: Who Framed Roger Rabbit? 54–5
syrups 14

tequila 13
    The Accidental Tourist 82–3
    First Aid Box 112–13
    Get Him to the Greek 94–5
    Lido Sour 104–5
    Mission Impossible 116–17
    Papaya the Sailorman 60–1
Teriyaki Manhattan 132–3
Thirst Aid 44–5
Tiger's Milk 122–3
tinctures
    base tinctures 24
    Salts of the Earth chlorophyll tincture 98–9
    Salts of the Earth Electric Avenue tincture 46–7
    Salts of the Earth Greek tincture 94–5
tomato consommé: Jugged Peas 130–1
tomato juice
    Little Miss Sunshine 128–9
    Rock Pool 124–5
    Tiger's Milk 122–3
truffles: Field Notes 40–1

venison carpaccio 108–9
vermouth
    Cherry Popper 110–11
    Strawman Proposal 114–15
    Teriyaki Manhattan 132–3
vitamin E capsules: lip balm 67
vodka 12
    Bandage of Brothers 64–5

base tinctures 24
celery bitters 23
Jugged Peas 130–1
Naughty Piglet 126–7
Pollen Count 52–3
R-2-Beetroot 74–5
Sazerac to the Future Pt 1: 88–9

Watermelon G&T 62–3
Werewolf of London 96–7
whisky/whiskey 12
    Ball Park Figure 42–3
    base tinctures 24
    Deer Hunter 108–9
    Field Notes 40–1
    Lost in Translation 134–5
    Sazerac to the Future Pt 1: 88–9
    Searching for Sugar Man 86–7
    Smoke the Weed 36–7
    Teriyaki Manhattan 132–3
white wine vinegar base shrub 20–1
    Cucumber Daiquiri 38–9
    Dr Greenthumb 56–7
    Parklife 48–9
    Pollen Count 52–3
    Werewolf of London 96–7
Who Framed Roger Rabbit? 54–5
wine, sparkling: Spritz 138
Wolfschmidt Kummel
    Bandage of Brothers 64–5
    Werewolf of London 96–7
Wonka Bar 78–9

You Can't Handle Chartreuse! 106–7

Zucca-Rabarbara: R+H+U+B+A+R+B 50–1

'At all times I have found Chris and Dave to be reliable, conscientious, courteous and most of all class innovators.' – Jillian Maclean M.B.E. and MD of Drake & Morgan

'Chris and Dave are two of the most inspirational and innovative consultant's I've ever had the pleasure of working with. They have the rare gift of being able to develop intricate and innovative drinks ideas and menus, maintain outstanding attention to detail and to deliver it all with a keen sense of fun!' – Johnny Neill, Owner of Whitley Neill Gin

'The best way to describe these lunatics is Acrobatic, Diplomatic & Charismatic.' – Alessandro Palazzi, bar manager and Martini Master at Dukes Bar in the Dukes Hotel

'I Throbbingly love Chris and Dave . . . they create amazing REAL venues with divine mouth marriage menus. All their ingredients are meticulously sourced with delight, pride and a true passion for everything that is served in their bars and restaurants . . . sensational food, ravishing cocktails. Always happy, always the best for their customers and all presented with a mischievous twist of elegant wit. They have a way of making you feel like the favourite version of yourself. Chris and Dave properly care about their customers and I utterly love them.' – Cleo Rocco, owner of AquaRiva Tequila

ABOUT THE AUTHORS & ACKNOWLEDGEMENTS

Chris Edwards and Dave Tregenza have spent over 25 years in the drinks industry. With senior roles at Adam Street Private Members Club, The Baltic, Northbank and Drake & Morgan. Using their combined knowledge and passion for new exciting cocktails and unusual ingredients, Chris and Dave created Salts of the Earth. Providing guidance and counselling on classic and bespoke cocktails, creating exciting new drinks menus for established brands and other venues, training sessions, pop-ups and events are just some of the services offered.

Salts of the Earth own neighbourhood restaurant and cocktail bar 'The Shrub & Shutter' in Brixton, and 'First Aid Box' a cocktail bar and restaurant in Herne Hill. 'Blinder' opened in the back of the First Aid box in 2016.

Both bars made the Top 10 ten bars in London for *Time Out London* and *The Bar Chick* and Top 5 bars in the World to Look Out For (The Shrub and Shutter) – *Condé Nast*, Gold Standard Bars 2015

A few previous clients include Drake and Morgan, Barrio bars, Baxter Storey, FM group, Saint Nick's, Red Bull, Schweppes, Made.com, Habitat, Snow Queen Vodka, Warner Edwards, Ballantine's whiskey, Twinings Tea and many more.

Chris and Dave were nominated for innovators of the year in 2016 in the IMBIBE magazine *Personalities of the Year* awards.

Thank You To:

The Edwards

The Tregenzas

The Pisarevskis

The Loxleys

The Overingtons

David Strong

Sammy Rosenthal

The Shrub and Shutter clan past & present

The First Aid Box clan past & present

Media Wisdom

Soho Wine Supply

Jillian Maclean

Masters of Malt

Doctor's Orders by Chris Edwards and Dave Tregenza

Published in 2017 by Hardie Grant Books, an imprint of
Hardie Grant Publishing

Hardie Grant Books (London)
5th & 6th Floors
52–54 Southwark Street
London SE1 1UN

Hardie Grant Books (Melbourne)
Building 1, 658 Church Street
Richmond, Victoria 3121

hardiegrantbooks.com

British Library Cataloguing-in-Publication Data. A catalogue
record for this book is available from the British Library.

ISBN 978-1-78488-137-5

Publisher: Kate Pollard
Commissioning Editor: Kajal Mistry
Desk Editor: Molly Ahuja
Publishing Assistant: Eila Purvis
Editor: Sarah Herman
Proofreader: Delphine Phin
Indexer: Cathy Heath
Cover and Interior Design: Nicky Barneby
Photographer: Giles Christopher

Colour Reproduction by p2d

Printed and bound in China by 1010